I Never Thought I Would Live This Long

Wayne Simmes

Published by Wayne Simmes, 2023.

While every precaution has been taken in the preparation of this book, the publisher assumes no responsibility for errors or omissions, or for damages resulting from the use of the information contained herein.

I NEVER THOUGHT I WOULD LIVE THIS LONG

First edition. May 4, 2023.

ISBN: 979-8223733638

Written by Wayne Simmes.

Also by Wayne Simmes

The Devil, The Ghost and Will Anderson
I Wish I Was a Cowboy
I Never Thought I Would Live This Long

Table of Contents

Title Page

I Never Thought I Would Live This Long

The Last 70 Years Through The Eyes of A Common Man

An Autobiography by Wayne Simmes

Author Wayne Simmes

Copyright Sept. 2011

Smashwords Edition

Disclaimer: The story is true to the best of my recollection. Now according to my children, my recollection has been hampered greatly by my association with Jim Beam. If they are right then this book would be hotter than anything that Harold Robbins ever wrote. Unfortunately, I have no memories of these sordid and risqué things they tell me about. This is not intended to be an exposé nor is it my intention of embarrassing anyone with this story. There are many embarrassing stories that I could tell about my children, but I figure that if they want those stories told they should write their own memoirs. It is also not necessarily in chronological order.

Prologue

The world has changed drastically since I was born in 1944. Look around you at all the electronics you have today and realize that almost none of those existed when I was born. There were no television sets or at least none that common people owned. There were no recording devices for video or audio. Radios were so big and heavy that you could not carry them around with you and even if you were strong enough you could only carry them as far as the cord would allow. There were no video games. TikTok was the sound that a clock made not an application for a computer that had not been invented yet. Social media was the interaction of children on the school bus or the playground.

Children had to amuse themselves by playing games with one another or by reading books. If you owned a record player it was likely one that you had to wind up before playing. You didn't just pop into

Wal-Mart to buy your groceries, clothing, hardware, pet food, or other miscellaneous items. There is a good chance that you had never heard of a TV dinner. Your milk was probably delivered to your door or you got it firsthand from a cow. For most people, they had never ridden on an airplane. Space travel was still only in the imagination.

If you had an electric washing machine it probably had two rollers that you fed your clothes through by hand for the water to be wrung out of them. There was always a chance of catching a body part in those rollers and having it pulled through. Thus comes the expression "getting your tit caught in a wringer." You did not throw your clothes in the dryer. You hung them on the line in the backyard and prayed it did not rain.

You got your news from a newspaper or by listening to the radio. If you did have the news delivered to your door it might be a couple of days late because it was probably sent by U.S. mail.

You learned what the weather would be by looking at the sky. "Red sky at night, sailor's delight, red sky in the morning, sailors take warning." Or one of my mother's favorites, "A fleecy sky never leaves the ground 24 hours dry."

Chapter-One I Wasn't Born In a Hospital

My life started on a risky note. There was still a little more than a year left in the Second World War when I was born in a house on a farm in the Western New York township of Randolph. I do not know why I was not born in the hospital either in Salamanca, New York or in Jamestown, New York. Perhaps it was because of financial reasons or perhaps the rationing of gasoline. In any event, old Doc Holton came out to the house with his big black bag and when he left with it there was another Simmes boy for the farm to support. My brother Bruce was three years old at the time and the story was relayed to me many years later that he was convinced that the Doctor had brought me in that big bag and left me with my mother.

I never considered the added risk of an at-home birth to my life expectancy until I began looking back at all the other things that went wrong in my youth.

Chapter Two-Toy Guns and Anti-Social Behavior

It is hard to believe in this day and age when children are expelled from school for putting two fingers together with their thumbs on top to emulate firing a handgun that there was a time when bringing toy weapons to school was an acceptable practice. On any given day you could find cap guns, wooden guns, toy swords, and rubber knives, which were brought to school as toys. And amazingly not one person was ever shot or stabbed by them.

Now I have to tell you that I have no memory of much of anything that happened to me during the first five years of my life. I am sure there are plenty of people that find that unbelievable but those folks may not have lived as long as I have. I wish that I had started a diary when I was six months old and then all this would be documented.

However, there are a couple of incidences that were told about me enough times so they stuck in my mind. One was when I was approximately three years of age. My brother Bruce who was three years older than I was had some of his friends over to play hide and seek. Somehow we ended up in the haymow. I had a large toy pistol with a long barrel and I was hiding behind some hay when George Wendell stuck his head over the hay mound and announced he had found me. I guess he regretted that immediately as I understand it I hit him over the head with that toy gun and announced, "You're out cold, I'm Gene Autry". And George later announced that he almost was too.

How true is that story? I really cannot say as everyone involved that day or who heard the original recital is dead. So there is no one left to confirm or deny it. One thing that bothered me years later, when my sister I believe again recalled it, was that it happened in our haymow. That mow was very high and the wooden ladder went straight up. The rungs were quite far apart and it seems unlikely that a three-year-old could have climbed it by himself. Of course, I suppose one of the older children could have helped me up there.

The other discrepancy was that I am sure it was told that George stuck his head up over a bale of hay. I was much older than three when we got our first hay baler. So it must have been a pile of loose hay.

Another incident occurred when I was in kindergarten. I had taken a double-barrel cork gun to school as a toy for recess. It was fairly heavy as it had metal barrels. For some reason, I had an altercation with the biggest boy in the class. Like the .45 caliber pistol was the equalizer in the old west, that cork gun was the equalizer in my kindergarten class. It seems I used it as a club to cut the bigger child down to size. I do not remember anything else about that occurrence and it might have gone unremembered except that years later I found one of my kindergarten report cards where my teacher had noted that I was perhaps too violent and that I sometimes hurt other children.

Now one might ask what was the punishment for such anti-social behavior. In all honesty, I do not recall. I do know that I was not grounded from watching television or from my favorite video games. We did not get our first television until some years later and there were no video games. I can hear the young people now. Horrors, how could anyone live without those necessities of life? We did have a huge old tube radio that my parents listened to Amos and Andy and the Lone Ranger on. Perhaps they restricted my listening for a time. Truthfully, the episode with George was probably just laughed off. The incident in kindergarten, not so much. I would not be surprised that I might have gotten my bottom tanned for that one. If so the tanning would have been administered by my mother. In all my years growing up, I never saw my father raise a hand to his children except once. And that was because my brother had disrespected my mother.

And just a side note, my father was not a hugger either. While I don't remember him ever physically disciplining me, I also don't remember him ever hugging me either. Perhaps that is why even to this day I find the idea of expressing myself by hugging someone other than my wife to be difficult.

Chapter Three-I Was an Angry Child

If the truth is known I have been angry much of my life. I cannot pinpoint exactly why that is but I can tell you that I got in more fights in school than the normal boy that attended a small country school should have. Most of them I do not believe I started but I never backed away either so the result was the same.

Sometimes it happened because I thought I was protecting a friend or someone that was picked on by a bigger kid. I would wade in and before you know it fists would be flying and when it was over I usually had won. But the strangest thing would happen the kid I thought I was protecting usually turned against me immediately.

Sometimes the fight would start over some trash-talking. I remember one time my old nemesis Frank Snow introduced me to a new kid that had started at our school. But the way he introduced him was to say how tough he was and how he was looking forward to seeing me get my ass kicked. So naturally, I had to prove him wrong, and before anyone had time to think the new kid was laying on the ground bruised and bloody.

I have no idea why Frank felt it necessary to test me with someone else. He could have whipped me on my best day and once he did just that.

The fights did not stop once I had left school either. I remember one time when I was out drinking with a few friends I had at a bar called "The Jericho". A guy that I didn't know asked me to give him a ride to Buffalo and that he would pay me $50 if I did. I agreed and when he got into the car I asked him for the money before I would get on the road. He seemed insulted that I did not trust a total stranger to do what he said that he would do.

I again asked for the money and he started swinging from the passenger's seat. Luckily for me, he took an overhand swing and he got more of the dome light than of me. I knew that only a fool tries to fight inside of a car so I quickly got out rushed around to his door and pulled him out and began hitting and kicking him until someone finally pulled me off before I did some permanent damage.

Somehow the word got back to my parents and they had mixed reactions. My mother was outraged not only because of the fight but because it happened in a bar parking lot. My mother did not believe in alcohol of any kind except for medicinal purposes. There was always a small bottle of whiskey in the cupboard to be administered a teaspoon at a time if someone had a stomach ache. I know that my father found the teetotaling to be a bore. I heard him say one time when we had pizza for dinner, "Pizza and no beer, oh hell."

My father, on the other hand, sounded kind of proud. That could have been because, in his younger days, dad was quite the scrapper himself. My grandmother told me a story one time of how dad and my uncle Frank (my mother's brother) got into an altercation with a half dozen men in a bar in East Randolph. They decided to take the fight outside and dad and Frank exited first. They stood on each side of the door, which was wide enough for only one person to pass at a time. As the six guys came out dad and Frank piled them up on the sidewalk ending the fight with no damage to themselves.

Another occurrence happened at a high school dance. That was just plain stupid when my friend, Ron dared me to ask a girl to dance. I was always one to take a dare and so I did not realize that the girl had a huge boyfriend. I went over and asked her to dance and she readily accepted. I am sure looking back that she wanted to make her boyfriend jealous and it worked.

As I stepped out the door of the gym he was there and confronted me. He told me that he had seen me dancing with his girl and he was going to beat the shit out of me. I told him I didn't think so and let one fly from my hip catching him squarely on the point of his chin. Most guys would have gone down and when he didn't I knew I was in trouble. I don't know how long we went at it but at some point, I could hardly breathe because I was so winded. So I took a couple of steps back and said, "If it is all the same to you I would just as soon call this a draw." He replied that he didn't agree and I hit him again. When it was all over I had a slight concussion and he had a broken jaw. That was the only fight that I was ever in where a doctor's services were required. Once again my mother was less than amused.

One kind of funny side note to this occurred when a friend named Carl John (they called him CJ) and I decided to go bowling one Sunday afternoon. CJ decided to drive and we took a back road so that CJ could show me where another boy's car had been taken the night before after he was in an accident. The junkyard was on the left-hand side of the road just before a railroad crossing. No lights were flashing and the barrier was not down but for some reason, a woman driving a full-sized Mercury had stopped just before the tracks. CJ was looking off to the left pointing out where Dale's car was and He never saw the stopped Mercury. The little Ford Falcon he was driving plowed into the rear end of that bigger vehicle at about 30 miles per hour.

Nobody wore seat belts back then and my head hit the windshield and for a few minutes, I could not see because of all the blood in my eyes.

At any rate, we finally made it to the Jamestown hospital and a doctor that had taken a large Muskellunge fishing lure out of my head a few years before patched me up. I had a huge turban around my head when CJ's father drove me home and helped me into the house. My mother took one look at me and exclaimed, "You've been fighting again!"

Chapter Four-Cement Walled Porches, Baseballs and Rocker Knockers

What does a child do when they cannot watch television or play games on their computers? For me, it was some form of baseball. I loved the game but it is a hard game to play by yourself. And so I improvised. I spent hours tossing the ball as hard as I could against first the ground and then catching it when it would bounce up off the cement wall of our front porch.

Of course, one cannot bounce a ball off a cement wall forever. That is why God created small rocks on the side of a gravel road. And of course, you need something for a bat. Ah, yes the scrap lumber from my father's sawmill. I would find a good piece of wood, whittle it down on one end for a handle and use it to hit those rocks over and over again. I was always Mickey Mantle so most of the rocks were deposited either in the farm pond or over it, which would be a home run.

I loved baseball, there just were not enough neighbor kids close enough to actually make two teams to play. And so I improvised by throwing and catching a ball and by hitting rocks, which I pretended were balls. My team was, of course, the New York Yankees. I am not sure why I started rooting for them. I was too young to have decided that they were my state's team. I imagine that I was following my brother's lead. But then he became a traitor in 1954 when he switched his allegiance to the Cleveland Indians.

But although I no longer watch or listen to baseball because I believe the sport has been ruined by free agency and huge money the one team I do occasionally check to see how they are doing is the New York Yankees.

It is amazing to me that today mediocre players make millions of dollars while in 1952 the highest-paid Yankee was Phil Rizzuto who made $52,000 and Mickey Mantle made a paltry $7,500. Back then most of the players played not for the money but rather for the love of the game.

I remember reading about Mickey Mantle when I was a boy. He won the Triple Crown in 1956 with a batting average of 353, 52 home runs, and 130 runs batted in. Before the start of the 1957 season, he went into the Yankee's front office and asked for a raise. They told him that they couldn't give him a raise. They wanted to make sure his year wasn't just a flash in the pan. In 1957, he did not win the Triple Crown but he did hit for a better average than he had the year before, batting 365. Present day: Aaron Judge just signed a 9-year 360 million dollar deal because he hit 62 home runs. I wonder if he will ever come close to those numbers again.

The next spring he again went into the front office and this time, he demanded a raise. They told him they couldn't give him a raise since he did not win the Triple Crown. He said, "Then I am going to hold out." They informed him that if he did they would trade him to Cleveland for Rocky Colavito. So of course, he did not hold out. He later admitted that if they had known how much he loved the game he would have played for nothing.

Years later I saw an interview with Reggie Jackson where he said that if it was not for the money he never would play a game.

It is disgusting to me to see people who could not have carried Mantle's bat making millions of dollars and filling their bodies full of steroids to do it.

At some point, I believe that those playing the game will price themselves out of the marketplace. It used to be that going to a game was a family affair. I remember when I was a kid I could go see the Jamestown Tigers play a doubleheader for 85 cents

Chapter Five-A Day in the Life of a Farm Boy

A day in the life of a farm boy in the 1950s was filled with hard work and responsibility. It started with an early wake-up call from my father, who would pound on the ceiling and my floor with a long-handled broom at 5:30 A.M. While it was tough to leave the warmth of my bed, there was no option to sleep in as there were many chores to do on the farm.

During winter, my room was almost freezing as the only source of heat was from a vent that allowed heat from the kitchen stove to rise into my room. After quickly getting dressed, I would shovel a path from the house to the milk house and then to the barn. In summer, the first chore was to go out to the pasture and bring the cows into the barn to be milked.

Once the cows were safely locked into their stanchions, it was time to go up to the haymow and throw down hay for their breakfast. With 38 head of cows to milk, each cow needed a third of a bale, and they also got grain from the grain room. While shoveling the grain, I had to watch out for barn rats, which were nearly as big as a cat.

After completing these tasks, milking would begin, and pails needed to be carried from the barn, across the road to the milk house. This process continued until around 7 A.M. when it was time for me to get ready for school. My mother left the barn about 15 minutes earlier to start breakfast, which was always a hot meal as cold cereal was not an option for farm kids who needed their energy.

Washing up in the morning was quick, as there was no shower in the farm house, and I would change into the one set of school clothes allowed per week unless they were soiled beyond repair. The school bus arrived at either 7:45 or 8:00, and the ride would take a minimum of 45 minutes and sometimes an hour.

When the bus arrived on time, I had about 15 minutes to collect my books for morning classes and spend some time with friends before school started. The bus left school in the afternoon at 3:15, and if everything went well, I would be home by 4:00. We had an hour to kill before dinner, during which I might spend time with my horse or dog while my older siblings had their own activities.

In the fall, I could stretch the hour to an hour and a half by grabbing my shotgun and heading to the nearby woods for hunting. Afterward, it was back to the barn to milk the cows again.

Without a television for the first ten years of my life, the evening was spent doing homework, reading, or listening to the Lone Ranger on the radio. As a teen, I didn't have a set bedtime but would feel tired by 10 or 11, and the routine would start again at 5:30 the next morning. Despite the hard work, it was a fulfilling life on the farm, filled with responsibility and a sense of purpose.

Chapter Six-Life Would Have Been Lonely, Except For Dogs and Horses

The picture below was taken in our front yard. My grandmother lived in the trailer that is in the photo behind me. The dog was named Mike. My brother had one from the same litter named Pat.

And yes I still bite my nails.

I am sure that for the first few years of my life that my brother and I were close. There was no one else to play with and our sister was much older than we were. Ann was in fact 11 years older than I was and she got married when she was only 16 so she was not really a part of the family circle once I started school. She did, however, take us to the movies on many Saturday afternoons.

It cost 25 cents to get into the theater and another 12 cents for popcorn so with a little searching of the sofa cushions it was not hard to come up with the money needed to go. Most of the shows were cowboy themes although I do remember seeing some of the great movies of all time as well, "The African Queen", "Gone with the Wind", and "Oklahoma" among others.

My favorite actor was Gene Autry and my brother liked Roy Rogers. I think my sister liked Randolph Scott as many of the movies we saw starred him.

This is a picture of my sister, her second husband, and her children.

So for a few hours on Saturday life was good. But most of the time when I was not doing farm work, I had to entertain myself. Fortunately, I always had a dog and for most of my youth a horse. They became my best friends and any time that I was feeling down in the dumps they would listen to my tales of woe.

Until I was about 13 my favorite horse was a Welsh pony named, what else, Champion. And just so you don't think my brother was left out he had a big Palomino, called Trigger. But I don't remember him spending anywhere near as much time with that horse as I did with Champ.

At some point, as has to happen with all pets, Champion got old and had to be put to sleep. My sister was raising horses and she had a young thoroughbred Morgan colt that she gave me. I called him Prince and he acted the part. He held his head up high like he was royalty and everyone and everything beneath him.

I didn't have any friends to speak of. We lived out in the country and the nearest neighbor with children was about a half-mile away. The only child they had that was close to my age was a girl and I didn't have time for girls.

Now I realize that a half-mile or even a mile is not a great distance. But you have to realize that back then in a farming community, you just did not show up and expect to play with somebody. It was assumed and rightfully so that everyone had chores that needed to be done.

In my family from the time I was old enough at around six years old, I was expected to help in the barn. And before that age, you were expected to do dishes and help with the housework. I imagine that today that would be deemed child abuse.

After I reached school age, the normal day started at 5:45 am when Dad would call me out of bed to help milk the cows. Many mornings I would pray that he would forget that I was there and just let me sleep but not once did that ever happen. At 7 am most of the work had been done in the barn and my mother and we kids would head to the house to wash up a little, have breakfast, and then the kids would catch the school bus at 7:45.

You notice I said wash up a little. There was no time for a bath and our house did not even have a shower so a sponge bath in the sink was all we got before climbing on a school bus with a whole bunch of other children that were in the same boat. I am sure that you can see why the city kids didn't sit too close to those of us who worked in the barns.

School let out at 3 pm and depending on which route the school bus driver took we either got home at 3:30 or quarter till 4. Dinner was served at 5. So there was a period of a little over an hour each day in which you could do other things. Of course, that depended on how much homework you were assigned by your teachers. But there were days when you knew you could get your homework done after you got in from the barn and before bed so that you could put it off until later. On those days when I had not started to hunt I spent with my horse. I could tell him all the things that had gone wrong during the day and he always listened without offering any advice.

We needed to start the evening milking by 6 p.m. each day and so during those months when the cows were turned out to pasture during the day, Prince and I would ride down, round up the cows, and push them towards the barn. In truth, Prince was such a good cow horse that I could have sent him by himself to bring the cows back to the barn but my father would have had a fit. Without a bridle in his mouth, that horse would have bit any cow on the butt that didn't move at his pace.

I remember one time when I was helping my father cut young cattle out of the woods pasture. Since they had been allowed to run wild all summer, they were a little difficult to herd. We had them almost to the gate when one of the heifers broke back for the woods. Without me even touching the reins Prince broke after that cow and at a full gallop. It was just getting dark at the time and the horse hit a low spot in the ground and went head over heels. His hindquarters landed in the middle of me and severely knocked the wind out of me. I was more scared than injured and I guess I must have been screaming at the top of my lungs. My father came up to where I lay, did a cursory examination, picked me up, put me back in the saddle, and told me to go home. Sympathy is a word in the dictionary.

I usually rode Prince bareback rather than taking the time to saddle him. In the afternoon that wasn't difficult as he was always gentle at that time of day. The mornings, however, were a different story. And especially if the night had been a little bit too cold for his liking.

On those occasions, you could count on having him buck for at least the first 30 seconds of your ride.

I just want to throw in a little something about school. I hear children say quite often that they hate school. I always have to ask why and many times the answer will come back that school is boring. I cannot understand that. How can learning new things each day bc boring?

I can honestly say that I loved going to school. Oh sure, there were classes that I liked less than others and there were teachers I liked a lot less than others. I did not get along with my high-school biology teacher primarily because she insisted on teaching evolution as a fact instead of a theory.

I know that some of you reading this will be saying well of course evolution is a fact. Then why do they call it the theory of evolution? I could not bring myself then nor can I bring myself now to believe that man evolved from the apes.

I suppose if I could see some half-man half-apes roaming around it might be easier for me, but there doesn't seem to be any such beast on the earth. In fact, scientists have never even been able to say for certain that they have found the so-called missing link. Every time they have tried to pass something like that off to us it has been proven to be a fraud.

Why is it so much easier to believe that man evolved from apes than to believe that an intelligent being created man just the way he is? Of course, if you believe in a higher power then you cannot at the same time put yourself up as the smartest thing in the universe.

I also had difficulty with Chemistry again because of the teacher. He was an old man with the last name of Mains. On the first day of class, he announced that half of us would fail his class anyway so we might as well leave now. And the way he taught that class was so unbelievably dull, I would not be surprised if half of us did fail. I never did fail a subject in high school but that class was as close as I came to failing one. Algebra was a close second.

Of course, my children will tell you that I am some kind of a nut that buys into all the conspiracy theories. And to some degree, they are probably right. I will admit that I am not convinced that man ever walked on the moon. I don't really have a good reason for that except that I have read some reports by skeptics that said the earth was out of position to the other stars in pictures taken from the moon.

But I do buy into most of the conspiracy theories more because I do not trust our government than for any other reason. There is no doubt in my mind that more than Lee Harvey Oswald was involved in the assassination of John F. Kennedy. If he had acted alone I don't think that a common thug like Jack Ruby would have been allowed to kill him before he had a chance to be questioned.

I believe that Lyndon Johnson was the only person that had anything to gain from the death of President Kennedy.

I know that our government fabricated evidence before going after Randy Weaver at Ruby Ridge and I have my doubts if they had any probable cause for what they did in Waco, Texas.

We used a tragic accident to start the Spanish American War and the Vietnamese did not fire on our destroyer in the Gulf of Tonkin.

I find it strange that if Timothy McVeigh did indeed set off the bomb that killed 168 people why he surrendered peacefully to a lone highway patrolman when he had a loaded pistol on the seat beside him?

Chapter Seven-I Hated Cows, but I Loved the Land

I liked almost everything about dairy farming, except the most important aspect. I hated cows. I believed that a cow was the meanest animal that God ever put on his green earth. Perhaps if I had not had to milk them I would have had a different view. But unfortunately, milking cows is how a dairy farmer makes his living.

I learned early on that when you stepped into a cow's stall to milk them that you could expect to be swatted with a tail heavy with whatever they picked up from the gutter. Next, when you bent down to put on the teat cups they would jamb you against the metal post. And if they did not kick you in the head they surely would step on your foot and grind theirs on top of yours.

But everything else involving farming, I enjoyed. And I loved the land. Our farm consisted of 224 acres of land, some of which were woodland and wood pasture. Small game was abundant and so were white-tailed deer.

Our old house was two stories painted white. It had three huge white pillars in the front that held up the porch roof. Four huge maple trees guarded the front and looking at that house from the front you could almost imagine that it was a plantation manor.

You can get a good idea of the size of that house. One interesting side note is that it did not have a central heating system. There were two stoves in the house, one combination of wood and electric in the kitchen, and a wood stove in the living room. In the winter both stoves were loaded first with wood and then with hard coal. In the morning they would be almost extinguished.

The upstairs was heated by opening a grate over the kitchen stove so that heat could radiate upwards.

It was not unusual in the winter to see the entire family bundled together around that wood stove in the living room.

Across the road to the left was a tool shed that was more than likely built to house an automobile but had been converted to the job of keeping the manure spreader and other farm implements out of the weather when they were not being used. The barn was off to the right and when I was little it did not have the milk house attached. Instead, you needed to carry the full pails of milk up and across the road where they were poured into large cans, which were, in turn, placed into a cold-water tank until they were collected by the milk truck that made a daily run.

In the back of the house were a variety of fruit trees. If you stepped out of the woodshed the first tree you would happen upon was a sour cherry tree that provided enough canned cherries to keep us in pies for the winter. Next was a peach tree and to the left of that three plum trees.

Finally, on the far left was a huge pear tree that had lost part of its trunk to a small tornado that had come through sometime before I was born.

Off to the right of the house was an orchard with another cherry tree and trees with every type of apple you could imagine. The most popular apples we had were called Northern Spies as they would keep through the entire winter down in our fruit cellar. So if you wanted a snack you could go down and munch away or if you wanted apple pie there were plenty of apples for that purpose. Hardly ever would a meal end without dessert in that house.

If that was not sufficient the woods were filled with blackberry bushes and wild strawberries grew in copious amounts.

In addition to the four maple trees in the front yard, there were many more adult maple trees in our woodlot. In the spring we would tap them and gather the sap. Our neighbor had a sap boiling station in the woods and everyone in the neighborhood would gather their own sap and take it to him. They would take turns helping cut wood for the fire and would help watch the syrup so that it did not boil down too much. In return, they got a share of the maple syrup produced.

Behind the apple orchard was an old town cemetery, which butted up against our property. I remember when I was 10 or so that some of us went and slept in that cemetery to prove our bravery. I also remember once when my brother and I went up to the neighbors to watch their new television on a Friday night. The program that was on was called. "Lights Out' and was about a mad scientist that kept a brain alive in a jar of fluid. The brain ended up taking over his mind and caused him to kill people. On the way home that night, I rode on the extreme left side of the road so as not to have to be next to that cemetery.

The next Friday night we again decided to go watch TV at the Walter's house. On the way there I rode on the left side of the road next to the cemetery. My brother informed me that I should be riding on the right side of the road. I informed him, "That is okay. I will ride on that side on the way back."

One of my favorite parts of living on a farm was doing haying. I remember a little bit about putting loose hay into the barn. The hay would be pitched onto the wagon with forks and then when we got back to the barn a large set of hooks would be lowered by a pulley system. The hooks would be driven into the stack of hay and the tractor would pull it up to the track that ran around the haymow and released wherever it needed to be. I wasn't old enough to grasp the entire concept but it was quite an engineering feat. And of course, when you wanted to feed the cows hay it had to be thrown down the hay chutes with pitchforks.

We were using a hay baler before I was too old and that is really the first I remember helping. As soon as I was old enough to reach the controls, dad taught me to drive the tractor pulling the wagon behind to be loaded with those bales. When I got old enough and strong enough, my mother took over driving the tractor and I was delegated to picking those bales up and putting them on the wagon. And finally, I graduated to being the one stacking those bales on the wagon, which was the toughest job especially when Dad discovered that he could hook the wagon directly behind the baler. Of course, every time the baler spit out a bale it would cause the wagon to jerk causing the load to shift. Even so one whole summer I managed to lose just two bales off of one load. I took great pride in that.

When I was little I received an allowance of 25 cents per week but as I got old enough so that my labor was actually worth something Dad paid me $20 every two weeks. Of course, when I got old enough to drive that barely covered my gas although I bought the gas from my father at 25 cents per gallon.

But during haying season Dad paid me an additional $1.25 per hour for working in the hay field. That was big money back there. In fact, after graduating, I had a job dumping tomatoes off a truck at the South Dayton Canning Factory which only paid $1.16 per hour.

We always finished our haying earlier than everyone else because Dad started earlier. So when we were done with ours I would offer my services to the next-door neighbor, Harold Walters. The first time I approached him he asked me how much per hour I wanted and I told him $1.25. He counter-offered with a dollar an hour but I held firm. If Dad paid me $1.25 I wasn't working for anyone else for less. Harold finally agreed but let me tell you I earned every cent of that money.

He pulled the wagon behind the baler and he drove in 3rd gear. That was much faster than what Dad drove and those bales came off onto that wagon almost faster than I could keep up with them. After every second load, Harold would offer me a drink of water and I learned quickly to never refuse that drink. If you did you wouldn't see the water jug again for two more loads.

Years later when Lloyd Lyke asked Harold for a reference for me he told Lloyd that I was the best worker he ever had. I suppose that was because one summer when I came home on leave I drove past his farm and noticed that he had three kids on the wagon doing the same job that I had done all by myself.

Chapter Eight-Two Buckets of Minnows and a .22 Rifle

When I was nine years old my father decided to dig out a large farm pond in a wet area close to our barn. He reasoned that having a water supply would lower his insurance costs. But for Bruce and I having a pond meant having a source of water to swim in and possibly to fish in.

The problem was where would we get the fish. There was a stream that ran through our property and Bruce and I figured we could catch some of the minnows and use them to stock the pond. So when we had a few minutes between farm chores we would set out on our bicycles with a couple of buckets. By using stones to build a wall we could choke off the creek enough so that one of the buckets would serve as a trap in the opening that was left. Then we would go up the stream, toss rocks into the water, and when the fish dashed into the bucket we would lift it up trapping the fish inside.

We would then take the second bucket and repeat the process until we had a good collection of live fish in each bucket. Then Bruce would put one bucket on each side of his handlebars and ride the fish home. This process went off without a hitch until someone in the neighborhood convinced us that there was a panther that had been sighted in the woods.

So of course, we needed something for our protection when we did our fish runs. My father owned a single-shot .22 rifle that Bruce was allowed to use for woodchuck hunting and so we took the rifle with us on a fateful Friday afternoon in May.

Everything went fine until we had two buckets filled with minnows and water. Bruce could not carry both the rifle and the fish and so he gave me the rifle to carry across my handlebars on the way home. I thought he had unloaded the gun and He thought that I had. And in this incident, an unloaded gun was very dangerous. We had only pedaled a few yards when my front tire hit a rut in the dirt road and the gun jarred off my handlebars. As the stock hit the road the gun discharged and the bullet went first through my crossbar on the bicycle and then through my left leg.

I have no idea what was going through Bruce's mind as he saw me lying in the road in an expanding pool of my blood but he took the only action he could. He picked me up in his arms and carried me home to get help. I have no idea how long it took him to get me there but then the real problem came to the light. The only person that was home was my aged Grandmother who did not drive even if there had been a car there, which there was not.

After a few phone calls located my parents who were three miles away at my sister's house. They came and took me to the hospital in Jamestown, New York some 17 miles away. Today that would only take about 15 minutes but back then there were no 4-lane highways and the roads were curvy and narrow.

I have no idea how much blood I lost but the doctor did say later that it was a miracle that the bullet had passed between the large bone in my upper leg and the main artery without hitting either one. Nor had the shrapnel from crossbars caused any major damage.

Just a side note: my parents were Jehovah's Witnesses and so a blood transfusion was out of the question.

I spent three days in the hospital receiving penicillin shots every three hours. Once I was released to go home our family doctor came out to the house to administer penicillin once a day for the next 30 days. Certainly, that would have been unheard of in today's medicine.

Another thing that probably would not happen today was my fourth-grade teacher, Mrs. Fargo bringing my homework to me every day at the close of class, taking it back, grading it, and bringing it back the next day. If not for her kind and generous assistance, I would not have been able to pass the fourth grade and move on with the rest of my class. I have always been grateful to her.

By all rights, my life should have ended on that day in May 1954.

Incidentally, we did eventually catch enough minnows to stock that pond. And amazingly enough, they grew to be quite big fish. Some of them were called horned dace which had beautiful pink bellies. Some that we caught years later were over 12 inches long. Others were what we called shiners that got to around 8 inches in length.

My brother-in-law would come over sometimes and catch a bunch of them and take them down to the big Conewango Creek to use for muskellunge bait.

A side story about that occurred one time when I accompanied Don and his Father Doc. Ingerson on one of those fishing trips. Don and Doc used old casting rods with heavy nylon lines and I used a closed-face spin-casting rig. Well, at one point everyone was trying to see who could cast the furthest and of course, since I was using a lightweight monofilament line my lure went much further than the other two. Doc, however, was determined to cast further and he reached back and flung his musky plug with all his strength. Unfortunately, it didn't go very far before burrowing into the back of my scalp.

Both Don and Doc did everything they could to pry that lure from my head. They even tried to twist it out with pliers. But eventually and through my screams of death, they decided to give up and take me to the hospital.

After the doctor surgically removed the plug he said that I was the biggest fish he had ever seen caught.

Chapter Nine-You Can Outrun Your Brother but not the Veterinarian

The next episode in the miraculous life and times of Wayne Simmes occurred three years later, also in the month of May. It was a Saturday morning and I was horsing around with my brother in our driveway. At some point, he began chasing me and I jumped on my bicycle and sped away from him straight into the path of the veterinarian's speeding station wagon. Another miracle occurred as the huge vehicle only caught the back wheel of the bike sending it spinning on its' front wheel.

I flew through the air and landed on my left wrist.

Another trip to the hospital in Jamestown occurred and this time, I came home the same day with only a broken wrist to show for another miraculous escape from the Grim Reaper.

I did get a new bicycle out of the deal because the one that got hit was twisted beyond repair. Because of my broken arm, I was not able to play softball in gym class and so the gym teacher decided to use me as the umpire. I quickly learned that the umpire is the most hated person on the field. No matter what I called, ball, strike, safe, or out, it was always contested. It did give me practice though as later when I had children of my own I umpired a lot of games both baseball and softball.

Chapter Ten-It is Better to Ride a Tractor Than Have a Tractor Ride You

It was three years later that I managed another near miss with death. It occurred in August, this time, six months after my brother died in an automobile accident just 10 days after his 18th birthday. My best friend Sandy Brown was going to come over to spend the weekend at my house. He lived about five miles from our house and that day he did not have any way to get to my house unless he walked, which he frequently did. But this day I figured I could just go pick him up on the family tractor. Fortunately, I chose to drive the smaller Ford Tractor instead of the larger Massey-Harris.

I had gotten over my fear of guns several years prior and I was carrying a 30-30-caliber rifle in a scabbard next to the tractor seat. As I drove I kept an eye out for woodchucks and crows. I was watching one crow fly into a field to my left and I took my eye off the road for a second or two. The tractor drifted to the right side of the road and the right wheel started to slide on the loose gravel. Not realizing that you should steer into a skid and not away from it I whipped the wheel to the left causing the tractor to slide off into the ditch. This threw me partway from the tractor seat and the rear wheel caught my right leg and dragged me underneath the wheel.

That should have been the end of this saga, however, the ditch was narrow enough so that most of the weight of the tractor was supported on the sides of the ditch. The tractor traveled a few feet more and then stalled. Somehow my rifle ended up beside me in the ditch and I fired a shot into the air hoping to draw someone's attention, which it did. A neighbor found me, called my parents and you guessed it another trip to the Jamestown hospital was undertaken.

Other than bruises the length of my right leg and a severely twisted back I was pronounced fit to go home.

The odds of dying from any of the above incidents would have certainly been high but the odds of dying from all three would have been enormous. And in fact, those were not the most dangerous situations I ever faced.

Chapter Eleven-Alcohol, Cigarettes, and Fast Cars

My brother and some older friends of his introduced me to beer when I was about 12 years old. We would go fishing and spend the night on the creek bank. Invariably someone would show up with a case of beer. I was not particularly fond of the taste but I drank some anyway just to prove that I was not a prude.

I never questioned the fact that the driver of the car on the way home the next morning was not fit to drive. Nor did I question my own ability to operate a motor vehicle under the influence of alcohol when I started driving myself.

I always looked older than I actually was so by the time I was 17 I could buy beer without anyone asking for my identification. Many of the local bars also served me in their establishments.

My first car wasn't much of a threat. I paid $100 for a 1954 ford V8. It lasted for about two days before we discovered that the real oil seal was gone and so was the oil. The engine seized up with the bearings and crankshaft destroyed. It took about another $125 for parts and with my father doing most of the work we got it back on the road. I immediately drove it into a ditch going too fast on a dirt road and it was out of commission again while we got a new fender and headlight from the junkyard. If I had been smart at that point I would have gone back to riding horses. Of course, that would have been difficult because I had sold my horse to get enough money to buy the car.

It became obvious that Ford would be more trouble than it was worth and so my mother helped me trade it in for a 1957 Pontiac.

Again it was a V8 but this time, the motor was working just fine. It had a 252 horsepower V8 engine and would top out at 110 miles per hour.

One thing that probably helped me get through my teenage crazy years of high-speed driving was that in New York State 16 year-olds could not drive after sunset without a parent or guardian with them. So for the first year after getting my license, I was only allowed to drive during the day and most days were taken up with either school or farm work.

I did manage to get a ticket for speeding one Sunday afternoon. In my defense, the town limit ran for a full mile out of town and they kept the speed limit at 25 miles per hour, which almost no one obeyed. But unfortunately, for me, a State Trooper caught me speeding up inside that before I got to the 50-mile-per-hour sign. I was taken in front of the town justice, fined $10, and threatened with the loss of my license.

I pled guilty and figured that would be the end of it but boy was I wrong. It seemed that every time I drove through town I would have a cop on my back bumper. Of course, the fact that my brother had died in a high-speed accident probably contributed to that.

In the following two years, I was stopped 26 times but only received one other citation. That might have cost me dearly if not for the town Justice of the Peace's mother being friends with my sister's mother-in-law. My last name was, of course, Simmes but my sister had taken her husband's name, which was Ingerson. So Justice Honey's mother did not realize she was divulging secrets to the enemy. It seems that this Justice of the Peace had decided well before my case came before him that he was going to fine me $500 and take my license.

The word was relayed to my sister and then to my parents. It was decided that the prudent course of action would be to retain an attorney and fight the case since I had already been found guilty in advance. I told my side of the story to the lawyer and he said not to worry about it since most of the time the cops failed to introduce evidence of speed limit signs being posted and seldom introduced a certificate showing that their speed-o-meters had been checked for accuracy.

When the trial began the police officer took the stand and told the story of how he followed me out of town and clocked me at 50 miles per hour but could not catch me to give me the ticket within the town limit. He also stated that he followed me for miles with his red light going and I refused to pull over.

On cross-examination, my lawyer asked him why if he clocked me at 50 miles per hour inside the town limits why he could not catch me. "Doesn't your car go more than 50 miles per hour?"

Although it was a clear violation of the town's policy for their police vehicles the cop had a friend riding with him that day and so he was called to the stand as well. He told a completely different narration of the events saying that I had pulled over as soon as the cop had turned on his lights.

At that point, the cop said, "I rest my case."

My attorney immediately stood up and said, "Your honor, I request that this case be dismissed because the police officer did not produce a certificate showing that his speed-o-meter was accurate nor did he even show that speed signs were posted."

The cop jumped up and said, "I have that information right here."

"That is too bad," remarked my attorney. "You rested your case."

"The Justice was furious. "I have no choice but to dismiss this case on a technicality but I know you're guilty."

My lawyer then began to dress down the Justice. "We had witnesses that we could have called but they were unnecessary because your prime witness didn't do his job properly. You have no cause to berate my client."

So how much did I save by retaining a lawyer? His fee to come the 20 miles from Salamanca to Randolph and try the case in Justice Court was $50.

Now I do not want anyone to think that I was being picked on unnecessarily. I did drive like a maniac and a lot of the time under the influence of alcohol. It is indeed a miracle that I did not wrap my car around a telephone pole or run into a bridge abutment similar to the one where my brother died. But for the most part, the cops never stopped me when I was speeding. It seemed they valued their lives more than my license and trying to catch someone driving more than 100 miles per hour on dirt country roads is taking your life into your hands.

But to show how desperate the police were to catch me doing something wrong, one night my best friend, Ron Sikes asked if he could drive my car. I said, "You don't want to do that. You will get stopped." He replied that he wouldn't get stopped because he wouldn't do anything wrong. So I kind of chuckled to myself and handed him the keys.

At some point on the main stretch between East Randolph and Randolph, we made a hard right-hand turn. It was just after you went over a bridge and you had to slow down to almost a crawl to make that turn. We dropped off a friend on that side street and then Ron pulled back out onto the main road and accelerated back to the legal limit of 35.

A few seconds later red lights came on behind us and Ron looked at me mystified before pulling over to the side of the road and turning off his engine. A Deputy County Sheriff came up to his window and without asking for any identification said, "Come on back to the car Wayne."

Ron looked at me and said, "You better come with me." So I got out and followed them back to the car. I got in the backseat while Ron got in the front on the passenger's side of the cruiser. The cop finally asked for the license and registration and when he looked at them he was totally confused. "You are not Wayne Simmes," He said to Ron.

"No, I am," I spoke up.

"Was he driving the car?" The cop asked. I know that sounds stupid since he had just requested that Ron follow him back to his patrol car but it just goes to show how surprised he was to find that the patsy he thought he was arresting wasn't the right patsy.

I acknowledged that Ron was indeed driving and he said to him. "Why were you going 60 miles an hour when you came over the bridge back there?"

I said, "He wasn't he was going 15 miles per hour."

"You shut up!" He raged. "Ron, I am going to let you go because I know your parents. But (looking back at me) I am going to get you."

One side point in this story was that I had never been on a date with a girl. My neighbor Barb was a year older than I was and so I asked her out to a movie one Saturday night, more to have a driver than a date. Before we got to the theater she made a left-hand turn across traffic and was almost hit by another motorist. We ended up on some church steps and though my car was not seriously damaged that was the last time I invited a girl out to be my chauffeur. I liked Barb, I just liked my car more.

Chapter Twelve-Anchors Away

Having no idea what I wanted to do with my life and approaching the age where I would have to register for the draft a friend and I decided to sign up for the Naval Reserves. We went in on the buddy system where supposedly you would get to serve your two years of active duty together. The only time we were ever together after our active reserve was over was during our two weeks of boot camp and that was only on the train coming and going. When we arrived at the Great Lakes, Illinois he was assigned to one company and me to another. We did not see each other for the entire two weeks. We also had to serve two weeks of active duty during the summer. I do not remember where he was sent but it was not with me. I was sent to the USS John W. Weeks, a destroyer out of Norfolk, Virginia. And when we went for active duty I was assigned to an aircraft carrier while he was assigned to a submarine. Some buddy system!

The only time in my life that I got seasick was on that destroyer. We ran into a heavy storm just off of Norfolk and the ship was rocking and rolling pretty badly. They had served greasy pork chops for dinner (I am sure on purpose since it was a training cruise) and the boson's mate on watch with me was puffing a big cigar in my face. I spent quite a lot of time that night bending over the rail.

My first month of active duty was served in the Brooklyn Navy Yards assigned as a Mess cook. One thing that I did learn was that Chief Petty Officers do not like their eggs with broken yolks. And they also expect that you will be able to crack an egg in each hand so as not to take too much time on any one breakfast. Fortunately, I was only there for three weeks because I never did get that part of the task down pat.

I remember vividly the first time that I saw my duty station for the next two years. It was the USS Essex, CVS-9 stationed out of Quonset Point, Rhode Island. When I arrived at the Shore Patrol Gate at the entrance to the base, I asked for directions to the Essex. "Straight down to the end of the pier." I was told. That was about a mile away and I was carrying a very heavy sea bag. I walked almost to the end of that pier and the only thing I saw was what looked like a huge building. So finally, I asked a sailor that was also on the pier if he knew where the Essex was.

"You are looking right at it," he replied pointing to that big building.

He pointed me to the gangplank and I made my way up to the Officer of the Day's station where I was assigned to the Gunnery Department. While I was doing my reserve portion of my enlistment a petty officer had told me that if I were smart I would tell whoever was assigning billets that I wanted to strike for Quartermaster.

So when I arrived at the Gunnery Office and a petty officer asked me what I wanted to strike for I told him, Quartermaster. He looked at me funny and told me that there were no Quartermasters in the Gunnery Department. He then asked me if I could type.

I had taken typing in high school although I would not have said I was proficient at it but I said, "Sure I can type."

"Sit down and take a typing test," He instructed.

"Would it be all right if I take off my pea coat first?" I asked.

"You can take all your clothes off if you can type." Was his reply. And that is how I began as a yeoman striker.

This is the motley crew that worked in the gunnery office on the U.S.S. Essex.

Far left is Richard Treziack, next to him David Disbrow, Eddie R. Brooks is seated, me in the back, and the last guy I think was named Poindexter.

Those same people served with me for most of my tour of duty.

And they taught me how to play pinochle. Many nights we would play until 2 am and then catch 4 hours of sleep before returning for another day's duty.

After learning a little about the ship and the duties assigned to Gunnery, I was grateful for that high-school typing course. The vast majority of people assigned to the Gunnery Department end up on the deck force. These are the folks that chip paint, clean decks, and heads, and do most of the grunge work. The only job classification that could be worse is the people that work in the engine room and are constantly cleaning the bilges.

There was another diving assigned to Gunnery call Fox Division. They were the ones that worked on the fire control radar. The yeoman were assigned to that division as well and when the Division Officer saw my general qualification test and arithmetic combination scores he did everything to try and persuade me to change to fire Control technician. I later found out that I had the second-highest score on the ship. But looking back, I am glad I stuck with Yeoman.

I had hardly settled into my compartment and started to learn the ropes of my job when the ship set sail for Cuba. It was barely after the Cuban Missile Crisis and tensions were still extremely high. So when we set anchor off the coast of Guantanamo Bay an extra watch was assigned called picket boat duty.

The idea was that half a dozen sailors in a small boat would constantly circle the aircraft carrier looking for frogmen that might be coming from the island to try and blow up the huge ship. The watches were broken up into two different time slots. Some of us were assigned for five straight hours while others were assigned four hours with three hours off and then two more hours on.

It was without a doubt the most boring duty you could ask for, and probably the most insane of tasks. I have no idea what we would have done if we had seen a frogman. Only the boson had ammunition for his weapon, the rest of us carried unloaded 30-caliber rifles.

Well, once an hour the boat would pull into shore to allow those who smoked to light up. I didn't smoke so I was forced to stay inside the boat doing nothing. I quickly decided that smoking was the way to go and so I purchased a carton of Marlborough Reds at the exorbitant cost of $1.00. It did not take me long to get hooked on the habit and before very long I was smoking two packs per day. It was best if you bought the cigarettes at sea because once you hit port the cost of a carton doubled to $2.

I also found that cigarettes had another value. There was a great black market for American cigarettes in most foreign ports. Of course, we were only supposed to take two packs of cigarettes ashore in foreign ports but if you put one in the inside of each of your socks you could stretch that limit a little.

I bought a camel bone chess set in Karachi, Pakistan for five dollars and two packs of Marlborough's.

That habit lasted for about five years. Then I quit for religious reasons for a few years and then started back up. If it were true that you lost a day of your life for every cigarette you smoked I should have been dead many years ago.

The Essex was known as "The Oldest and The Boldest", having been in every major battle of the Pacific in World War II. She was also known as a ship that was constantly at sea. And so I did not spend a whole lot of my time in port. In my two years aboard that carrier, I visited Cuba twice, Halifax, Nova Scotia twice, Spain, France, Great Britain, Italy, Sicily, Malta, Egypt, Pakistan, Denmark, and probably several other places that I do not remember at the moment.

Most of the time being on the Essex was almost like being on dry land. It was so huge that unless the sea was particularly angry it didn't rock and roll much. But when we were coming back from our Mediterranean cruise there was a hurricane in the North Atlantic. Normally the sane and sensible thing would have been to stay inside the mouth of the Mediterranean Sea until the storm had passed. But not Captain West. He was determined to get the Essex home on time for Christmas and so out into the North Atlantic he ordered us to go. We were still several days away from homeport when we ran smack into that storm. Now the Essex was rolling so badly that they had to take the tables out of the mess decks. When we would go to chow we had to sit on the deck to eat our food. There was a lot of water floating on that deck. When the ship would roll away from us the water would flow away and when the ship would roll back all that water would come back to us and splash over us and whatever food we had on our tray.

The second night I was sleeping in my bunk on what was called the 02 level, just below the flight deck when someone started shaking me and telling me to get out of the compartment. I could smell fumes exceedingly strong and I asked what had happened. Well, it seems that our 50-ton radar mast had fallen onto the flight deck crushing two jet planes underneath it. Those planes were fully fueled and the jet fuel was flooding all the birthing compartments below the flight deck. So for the rest of the night, I stayed inside the Gunnery Department Office many decks below.

To understand the next paragraph you need to know that The Essex was an extremely old aircraft carrier, having been commissioned in 1942 and having fought in every major battle of the Pacific after that time. She was also the first aircraft carrier to circumnavigate the globe, and the first aircraft carrier to go through the Suez Canal. She had logged more miles at sea than any other aircraft carrier up to that time.

At some point that same night, we developed cracks below the waterline, and our boilers flooded out so that we were dead in the water and unable to turn our bow into the storm. An old Boson mate came into the office and immediately made us all feel better. His comment was, "I have never heard of an aircraft carrier sinking because of rough weather, but this is probably another Essex first."

At one point we ended up in the eye of the hurricane and the seas calmed enough so that we were able to dump our trash off the back of the ship called the fantail. A couple of us went up to do that and we watched the only destroyer that had stayed with us. The others being much faster than the Essex had made a run for home. But the Blandy stayed behind for pickup duty in case someone needed to be rescued at sea. It was amazing to see that ship rolling even on the relatively calm seas. The ship would roll and her radar mast would touch the water on one side and then she would roll the other way and her mast would touch the sea on the other side. I cannot fathom how those sailors on that ship were even able to function.

And of course, it was silly to have that ship stay behind. I asked the Gun Boss what they would do if someone actually fell overboard in those seas. His answer was, "We would write your parents a nice letter."

When we finally pulled into the Brooklyn Naval Yards for repairs, we had taken on more damage than the ship had endured during the entire Second World War. Our radar mast was gone, our catwalks were gone and we had multiple cracks below the waterline. The ship that never stayed in port for more than six weeks did not sail again for over three months. They probably should have decommissioned her instead of doing the extensive repairs but shortly before I had been assigned to her she had been completely overhauled from an attack carrier to an anti-submarine warfare carrier. the straight flight deck had been changed and an angle flight deck was added. I am sure that they did not want to waste all the money that it took to refit her.

Except for that fateful Mediterranean cruise, nothing very, noteworthy happened during my two years on the Essex. Everyone had a battle station and mine was a phone talker on the 07 level. That meant 7 decks above the flight deck. It was also two levels above the bridge. To give some perspective, each level would be slightly higher than the floor of a normal building.

Any time that battle stations would be called I had to climb up a steep ladder to get into position, put on my headphones, and be prepared to relay information from the Gun Boss to the Captain on the bridge. The same thing was also true any time we took on fuel from a tanker or gave fuel to one of our destroyers. That was quite a sight to see us pull alongside those huge tankers and then watch as they shot a line over to our ship so that we could pull those huge hoses into position.

The reverse took place when we would give some of our fuel to our destroyers. It amazes me looking back how in even rough seas we never collided with one of those other ships. Our sister ship the U.S.S Lake Champlain didn't fare nearly as well as she collided with one of her destroyers while refueling and did enough damage that she was put out of commission for a while.

One thing that was kind of interesting is that every year we had to go through an operational readiness inspection. During those cruises, we had to practice shooting at targets with our four five-inch guns. This would be done either by shooting at a metal sleeve pulled behind an airplane or shooting at a barge pulled behind another ship. Fortunately, for the planes and the other ships, they towed the target a long way behind them because we never could hit those things. The plane or other ship would have been in as much danger of being hit as the target.

In most cases, if we could cause a burst within a thousand yards of the sleeve or a thousand yards of the barge we felt pretty good about ourselves.

On one such cruise, off the coast of Cuba, the loudspeaker came on when we were not expecting a drill. "This is not a drill, this is not a drill. General Quarters, General Quarters. All hands man their battle stations."

In record time, we got to our positions. I had just got my headset on when I heard. "Unidentified aircraft coming in off the port bow. Load."

Well, that scared the bejesus out of me for two reasons. First I knew we couldn't hit anything with our guns so if it was an enemy aircraft we would probably be sunk and second it must be real because the only way to unload a five-inch gun is through the muzzle.

It turned out to be one of our jets that had communication problems.

The hardest part of operational readiness inspections, for a yeoman, was that everything that happened during the day had to be recorded and typed up that night. Most nights during those cruises the four yeomen would still be typing at 4 am.

Chapter Thirteen-Sex Education or Lack Thereof

I had been on two real dates in my life when I met Janice Shenefiel. The first of those dates was with my neighbor Barbara Walters and the second was an afternoon bowling with a girl named Dawn. Neither of them had been spectacular enough that I wanted to try for a second date with either girl.

My best friend at the time Sandy Brown was dating Janice's best friend whose first name also happened to be Sandy. For some reason, they decided that it would be a good idea to try and get Janice and me to go on a date.

I had no idea what to expect when I picked her up at her house. I guess I should have because as I am fond of saying now that we have been married a few months shy of 50 years I met my wife when we slept together in Kindergarten. That is, of course, an absolutely true story.

Everyone was required to take a midday nap in our Kindergarten and the class was short a few cots so some of us had to share. Since Janice was the smallest girl in the class she ended up sharing a cot with me.

I am sure you can all see that we were destined for each other. I was in the bottom row fourth from the left and Janice was in the second row second from the right. And just look at those stylish clothes we were wearing. That is an interesting thing that many would not believe today. I was allowed two sets of clothes and they were expected to last the week. One set of school clothes that had to be folded neatly and put up when I got home from school and a set of clothes to be worn for play or work in the barn.

Our school system was also a split school meaning that some of the students went to a school downtown called the little school and others went to a school up on the hill called the High School or the Big School. After Kindergarten, Janice did her grade school at the "Big School" and I did mine at the "Little School". So we were never again in class together until junior high school. I did remember her a little bit from geometry class but at that point in my life girls were the least of what I was thinking about. Today I hear her say that I was the smart kid in that class. It is a good thing that she wasn't in my algebra class. She would be saying I was the class dunce.

At any rate, when she got into my old ford, she put me right at ease. I expected she would try to bore a hole in the passenger side door but she didn't. She sat close enough to talk comfortably but far enough away so that we were not touching. She was easy to talk to and at the end of the night, I walked her to the door and asked her for another date for the next week. She quickly told me she was busy that night and I figured that would be the end of it. I don't know how long I waited to call her again but at some point, we actually had date number two and that was when I fell madly and irrecoverably in love with her.

Through the years, I have sometimes not liked her very much but I have always loved her with a passion that will not die.

I went into the Navy that December and so we did not see a lot of each other for a while. I did, however, write her letters almost daily and she would write back occasionally. I went home every time that I could get a weekend pass and most of those weekends we would go out someplace. We dated like that for a year and a half before I finally asked her to marry me. A year and three months later we were married in a small ceremony at her parent's home.

I will never understand how I got such a hot chick.

Nine months to the day later, our first child, Robert was born. I guess we should have listened closer in sex education class. Oh, that is right they didn't teach that subject when we were in school.

It is strange though each of our children was born just three years apart from the one previous.

This picture was probably taken just before we left for our honeymoon. The family shot would have had to be taken a few years after we moved to Malone, New York since the youngest (Matthew in the middle) was born in Malone. Dig the mustache man!

Chapter Fourteen-I Learned to Hate Unions

There was not a whole lot of work available when I got out of the service. I even thought of applying for unemployment insurance but when I went in to apply they told me that I had to be out of work for two weeks before they would start the process. I thought what is the point, and started looking for work. I never drew a day's unemployment in my life. That must seem strange to people today since there are so many people receiving some type of government benefits that employers are having trouble finding workers. The Democrats say that we need immigrants to fill those positions, but I believe we just need to stop paying people not to work.

I put in applications at every place that I could think of or any place that had an ad in the paper. There was one job I wanted, an office position for a company in Jamestown, New York. But it was not available immediately when I got out of the Navy.

I finally found a job as a maintenance man working for the Randolph Seed Company. It was an old building and much of my work was simply cleaning and repairing. But one thing I was assigned to do caused me to think that I did not care much for the way the outfit was run.

You may know that seeds get old and do not grow well after they have sat on store shelves for just so long. So when they reached what we would call a sell-by date today, the stores would return them to the company for credit; and purchase new seeds.

Well, I had not been at the company very long when they told me my task for the next few weeks would be to cut open all those returned packages and repackage them so that the stores that had returned them for being out of date could buy them again.

I quit shortly after that and reapplied to the Office in Jamestown only to be told the owner of the seed company had blackballed me.

Well, I was out of work again and started the process of putting in applications anew. I told everyone that I would work any shift any hours and for any pay. And still, no one hired me. Finally, I started applying at companies 30 or 40 miles away from Randolph and I put in an application to Acme Electric Corporation. I had all but given up on finding a job and for some reason when they asked what shifts and hours I would work I told them I would only accept work on the day shift.

Lo and behold, two days later they called and offered me employment.

So the following Monday morning I reported to work an hour late as my alarm clock had failed to go off. I figured that would be the end of that stint of work but it wasn't. I don't know if they needed help that badly or if they just saw something in me but they excused me and told me to try not to allow it to happen again.

I was sent out on the line to work with another member of the crew and I found out that my job would be to wind transformer coils. Automated machines did some of the work, but the larger coils all had to be wound by hand on a lathe.

It was hard tedious work but I soon found that I was fairly good at it. And you had to be good to make any money. The base pay was two dollars 16 cents per hour. Since the job was piecework you could make more money if you could wind more coils than the daily rate.

Then the union rep came by and had a little chat with me and explained that I was never allowed to wind more than 150% of the daily rate. That was because if you made too much money on any one set of coils the company time study people would come out and raise the rates. Well, that went against my grain a little bit but I abided by what I figured was the rule that everyone must follow.

And then I got put on a run of coils where the daily rate was only 8 per day. And the order for that coil was over 5,000 coils. So naturally, I was working on that order for a long time. So after just a little while I was winding my 150% or 12 coils per day and I was getting done earlier and earlier every day but I still had to look busy or the foreman would call me out for not working. So I would take an inordinate amount of time braising leads for the next day's run and then for the day after's run. Well after a while it was to the point of stupidity so I wound an extra coil, which drove my percentage to 165%. I never went over that figure although I easily could have but one of the other workers reported me to the union and all hell broke loose.

The union steward came to me and demanded that I slow down. I told him that I could not in good conscience do that and he informed me that if I didn't someone would be waiting in the parking lot to do me physical harm. Well, I was a pretty big man and I figured that I could handle anyone that wanted to take me on but the Steward told me it would not be just one man that the entire line wanted to kick my ass.

So I did the only thing that I could think of to do. I went to the line supervisor and asked to be taken off of that run of coils. He told me he would not do it and I told him that if he didn't I would quit. So he left me and came back a few minutes later and showed me the Union Steward's time card from the day before. That S.O.B. had turned in 180% for his day's work.

I walked down the aisle and in a voice loud enough for everyone present to hear I announced. "If you want to see a rate broken I will show you how to break one. I wound 200% the next day, 250% the day after, and 300% the next day. Well, you better believe that Time Study was on the line the following day watching everything that I was doing.

Of course, I told them that if they raised the rate I would quit. I said no one could wind more than the present rate unless they were assigned to that coil for a very long time and found some way to make it easier, which I had. And then I showed them how adding just one strip of tape more than what the specs called for made the process much faster.

Well, they did raise the rate anyway but not by enough to piss me off so I didn't quit. But I did start receiving more threats every day and they even threatened to slash the convertible top on my car. I finally developed ulcers so bad that I thought I was having a heart attack.

I went into the employment office and gave them two weeks' notice. When asked why I told them the truth that working on a union line was doing more detriment to my health than it was worth. They agreed to transfer me to another plant where I could work at a straight hourly rate with no piecework.

I took the transfer but my ulcers were still acting up so I went to the Doctor and he gave me a prescription for Phenobarbital. That is wonderful stuff. I would be driving down the road, someone would cut me off and I would think that's okay, I don't care. The problem was that I quickly developed a reaction to the drug. It caused me to have severe hives on the palms of my hands and the soles of my feet. They would get so bad that I would have trouble walking by the end of the day. Some nights I would not be able to walk when I got out of my car at home and I would crawl into the house on my hands and knees.

I think I stayed with that company for another year. I was selling life and health insurance part-time and when it appeared I could make more money doing that than winding coils I finally quit.

I hate unions to this day.

Chapter Fifteen-The Greatest Salesman I Ever Knew

His name was Lloyd Lyke. I met him shortly after I had gotten married in 1965. He sold insurance to people in rural Cattaraugus County in New York State. He had a few small policies with my wife's family and one time when he was there visiting he asked if they knew anyone that might make a good insurance salesman. My father-in-law mentioned my name and said that I might be a prime candidate since I argued about everything. I guess he thought debating and sales went hand in hand.

Well, Lloyd looked me up, and after trying without too much success to sell me some insurance he talked to me about possibly becoming an agent for Farmers and Traders Life Insurance Company. They were called agents rather than sales representatives because they were classified as self-employed rather than employees of the company.

I was winding transformer coils for a company called Acme Electric Corporation in Allegheny, New York and I wasn't making all the money in the world. In my first year, I made $4800 and I figured that I would be rich if I made $10,000. So I figured that maybe I could make a little bit selling insurance in the evenings or on the weekends.

And so Lloyd dropped off the training materials for me to study for my insurance test. I don't know exactly when I got those materials but I do know exactly when I took my test to become a life and health, insurance salesman. It was January 20th, 1966. I know that because it was also the day my father died of a heart attack. He had gone out to the barn to feed the cows and never even got his coat off before he was struck by a massive heart attack and died on his feet.

Back then there was no way to reach someone unless you knew the specific location they were at and so my wife had to wait until I got home to give me the news. I was so excited as I walked in the door because I knew that I had aced that test. I was gushing about it until I noticed the silence of everyone in the room and I knew something was wrong.

One sad note to that story is that dad died without any life insurance. He had several accidental death policies, which were worthless at the time of his death. I guess he always figured that the farm and acreage were his insurance. Unfortunately, when you have to sell a farm the price goes way down.

I did not know anything about sales when I passed that test. The only advantage I had was the company had a nice canned sales pitch in a colorful folder called "You'll Earn a Fortune". Neither Lloyd nor his boss (who was also his brother-in-law) Bill Pawling used it but for me, it was a godsend. I spent hours with that brochure until I had every word and every word inflection down pat.

What I did not have down pat was the courage to knock on doors. Even though Lloyd showed me how to get leads from the local paper so that I would have a reason for calling on folks, for the most part when I knocked I was praying that no one would come to the door.

Lloyd helped me as much as he could but it wasn't long before he adopted the sink-or-swim approach. And so one Saturday I found myself all alone in Portville, New York knocking on doors. I am sure that I was close to giving up on the idea of ever making money, by selling insurance when I timidly knocked on a door. How they heard me I will never know but a man came to the door and asked me what I wanted. I told him that I represented Farmers and Traders Life Insurance Company and that someone said he might be interested in life or health insurance. "I am not interested in life insurance," he began.

"But what do you have in the line of supplemental health insurance?" He invited me in and an hour or so later I left with an application for a small health insurance policy. That sale probably saved my career in sales.

Now back to the greatest salesman I ever knew. Once I got to the point where I had enough leads so that it paid him to let me tag along, Lloyd would allow me to go with him perhaps once a week. I was always amazed at some of the things he was able to pull off that I could never have. I remember one evening when we were between appointments and Lloyd decided that we should not waste our time. So he said we should do some cold calls. Any good door-to-door salesman can tell you that knocking on a door without having a specific reason for being there is extremely difficult. Well, that night Lloyd decided to show me how it was done.

At the first house, we came to, Lloyd gave the door a good loud rap with his knuckles. A middle-aged woman came to the door, took one look at Lloyd's briefcase, and in a loud voice announced "I am not interested," and slammed the door. Well, I figured that was the end of it and turned to head back to the car. But not Lloyd. He put out his hand and stopped me and then told me to follow him. He led the way to the back door and again rapped loudly. The same woman opened the door and looked at us with total disbelief. Lloyd then said, "You know ma'am you have the meanest maid in town."

I almost broke out laughing at that point even though the door immediately closed with a loud bang. So I figured if Lloyd could do it so could I. So I took the next house and knocked loudly. Another woman came to the door and I said. "Good evening ma'am, we represent Farmers and Traders Life Insurance Company and one of your neighbors said that your husband might be interested in life or health insurance."

She looked at me with less than approval as she answered, "I suppose he might be. If he was alive." And again the door closed loudly.

To be honest, with you, I never did master the art of cold calling. I think that was one reason that I eventually gave up selling insurance. There were only so many leads to be had from the local paper and every salesman was working them. So if you could not fill out your day with cold calls eventually you ran out of people to talk with. Of course, we did ask everyone that would talk to us, who else they knew that might be getting married, buying a house, or having their first child.

Another example of Lloyd's sale prowess took place while we were working on what we called a salary savings case. Farmers and Traders had come up with a system where a small company could deduct a portion of an employee's pay to be used to buy insurance. The only stipulation was that we had to get 5 or more employees to agree to the plan. Theoretically, we were supposed to use high cash-value life insurance and point out how much the employee could save. The hardest part of the program was finding that small business where the owner saw the value enough to agree to the small expense of doing the payroll deduction.

Well, Lloyd and I found a vegetable packing plant and pitched the idea, and got approval. We were given a list of employees and addresses and we immediately started making calls to them. Lloyd decided that he would make the pitch to the first person on the list. And so when we got to the door Lloyd knocked and a man came to the door. The man took one look at Lloyd and remarked. "I know you, you sell insurance."

"No sir," Lloyd replied. "I sell savings."

"No, I do know you and you sell insurance." The man was adamant.

Again Lloyd replied. "No, I sell savings."

The man sighed and said, "That is too bad, I need insurance."

Lloyd looked him straight in the eye, did a military twirl on the point of his toe, and said, "I have the best insurance on the market." And he proceeded to go into the house and sell the man a policy.

No way could I ever have gotten away with that.

Another of the employees on that list was a young man who was the sole support of his widowed mother. These folks did not make all the money in the world but we asked each one of them how much they could save out of their weekly paychecks if it was taken out before they saw it.

Well, when we were in that house Lloyd immediately deduced that if something happened to the young man, his mother would be in dire straits, so he decided to pitch life insurance rather than savings. He asked how much the man could save and was told about $2 per week. Instead of just taking four weeks in the month Lloyd pointed out that there were 4.3 weeks in the month, which would be $8.60. Using that calculation and putting together a combination of permanent insurance and term insurance Lloyd managed to come up with a policy for $10,000.

When he showed the figures to the man and his mother, the mother exclaimed, "10,000 dollars, what good would that do me?"

Without any warning, Lloyd turned to me and said, "Turn off the lights, Wayne."

I obeyed and the room went dark. And then I heard something scratch and the room lit up with light. Lloyd had produced what we called a farmer's match and lit it. "Turn the lights back on Wayne."

"That is the difference, ma'am. The difference between a little bit of light and total darkness." Of course, they bought the policy.

After I had sold insurance full-time for a year, Bill Pawling, the regional manager made me a District Agent. That created a little bit of tension between Lloyd and me as up to that time he had been getting an override off of my sales. I think it was only about 5% but I was the number 7 agent in the company so my sales added substantially to his income.

Lloyd was also quite a joker. Many years later he hired me back to sell insurance for him in Franklin County, New York.

We had purchased a house in a little place called Constable, New York. It was an old beat-up place but we could buy it for cash and since I didn't know how successful I might be at making money in the middle of the north it seemed to make sense at the time. We had some friends from Pennsylvania that came up to visit us our first fall there. The wife's name was Calla and somehow she had heard that there were wolves that lived in that area. Some bushes grew up right alongside our house and when the wind blew them against the old metal siding it would sound like something was scratching trying to get in.

The first morning Calla got up and told us that she had not been able to sleep at all the night before because she could hear some animal, probably a wolf, scratching trying to get into the house. She was positive that if she went to sleep she would be devoured.

I tried to put her mind at ease by telling her that there had not been one case of a wolf attacking a human being in the continental United States, since before 1900. And it worked until Lloyd showed up a little later that morning.

She asked him about wolves in the area and I immediately broke in with the sage wisdom that I had imparted to her earlier.

Lloyd got a big grin on his face and then made it disappear. He turned to Calla and said, "There are two things you have to remember about that. One, no self-respecting wolf would ever report it if he did attack. And second, the law of averages would say."

Chapter Sixteen-Deer and Automobiles Don't Mix

Looking back, it flabbergasts me that when I was driving home as a stupid kid at speeds just below a supersonic airplane I never hit a deer. One insurance company estimates that there are over 63000 deer killed each year on New York State roads and highways and I will bet a lot of them happen in Cattaraugus and Allegheny Counties. By all rights, as many miles as I covered in the black of night, I should have hit at least one. And at the speeds, I drove if I had, I imagine it would have been the last thing I ever hit.

But low and behold I was well past my high-speed driving before I hit my first deer. It happened one night as I was on my way home from selling insurance. I saw a blur in front of me, felt a hard thump, and knew that I had just hit a deer. It was a little button buck and the only damage to my old small mercury was that it put out one of my headlights. The deer did not fare as well.

The second deer that I hit was the night my daughter was born. I was coming back from the hospital in a pouring rainstorm when once again I saw a blur in front of me. This time, however, my car did not come out of the encounter with just minor damage. The hood flew open and came back up over my windshield. It was amazing that I was able to get the car to the side of the road since I could not see anything.

I did not even try to find the deer that night. I just closed the hood and hoped it would stay down while I nursed the car home. The impact had driven the fan through the radiator and the final bill was $535. Today it would have been in the thousands of dollars.

I did find the deer the next day. It was a nice six-point buck but of course, that was too late to take the meat.

I have had many other close brushes with deer but those are the only two that I hit. My wife, however, added a few to her tally one morning when she was on her way to work. She was working in a nursing home and usually left the house around 4 am.

That morning, shortly after she walked out the door I heard our phone ring. I picked it up and said hello and all I could hear on the other end was crying. I finally figured out what had happened and got in the company truck that I drove to go pick her up. She had gone through a whole herd of deer and pretty much totaled our 1967 Galaxy 500 convertible. Thankfully she was not hurt seriously, just badly shaken up.

Later that day Lloyd came over to work with me selling insurance. When I showed him the spot where Janice had hit the deer, he remarked. "I have to hand it to her. She had to go all the way over to the other side of the road but she got those suckers."

Years later when I lived in Mannford, Oklahoma my daughter bought me a gadget to stick on my front bumper. It was supposed to warn deer that a car was coming but from many near misses I had traveled between Oklahoma City and Mannford each day for a year, I doubt that it worked.

Here in Ohio where we live in a residential area, we have deer cross in front of us all the time. And now and again we will look out our front window and see two or three deer standing in the neighbor's front yard.

Chapter Seventeen-From Salesman to Janitor

As I mentioned earlier, I had a hard time cold calling and at some point, I ran out of leads. My income suffered and so I mentioned to my mother that I needed to find a part-time job. The employment market was tight at that time and jobs, full or part-time; were scarcer than a hen's teeth. But my mother was a member of the Olean Congregation of Jehovah's Witnesses and another member of the congregation owned a small cleaning business. His name was Fred Higley and the company's name was Fred's Contract Cleaning. My mother mentioned me to Fred and he agreed to put me on part-time cleaning supermarket floors. He asked me if I could run a floor-cleaning machine and I told him sure I had done a lot of floor buffing when I was in the Navy.

He kind of chuckled and showed me what he was talking about. It was a large self-propelled machine that laid down cleaning solution, scrubbed the floor, and then vacuumed the dirty water back up. In actuality, it was much easier to handle than a buffer so it was not a problem.

Fred assigned me to help a young man on the floor-cleaning route. We would put all the equipment into a van and then drive to various locations and clean and wax the floors. Usually, we did about three different supermarkets in one night. Everything went fine for the first couple of nights as I was getting the hang of how everything worked. But the more I got accustomed to doing things the less work the other man did. It was almost as if he expected that he could just supervise while I did all the work.

So at some point, I discovered that once the equipment was unloaded I did everything else while he wandered around the store. So I figured if I was going to do all the work any way why did I need someone with me? And so without authorization, I fired him.

Of course, the next day he complained to Fred and I was called into the office to explain. So I told Fred exactly what was transpiring and low and behold he agreed with me. So he appointed me as the lead worker and hired another person to help me out. Again the helper turned out to be completely lazy and after a few nights, I fired him as well.

Fred was not as amused this time but after I explained that I did not need a helper to do the amount of work that we had he seemed pleased that he did not have to pay two people for a one-person job.

I was extremely good at making sure those floors shined and I got a lot of compliments from the store- owners. So Fred set out to teach me some other aspects of the business starting with how to clean carpets. In the beginning carpet cleaning was done with a buffer with a tank on the handle to hold the solution. It took some getting used to because when the handle was lowered into the position you took a lot of weight, which caused some back strain. If you remember I injured my back severely when I was 15 years old by being run over by a tractor. But I did get away with running that machine and became proficient with it for a few years.

I learned excellent work habits from my father and mother from working on our farm and it was not long before I stood out as the best employee that Fred had. But still, it simas a complete surprise when he went away for a few days to a conference and returned and called me into his office.

He sat me down and explained that at the conference they mentioned that anyone who could not bring themselves to fire unproductive employees should find someone that could. And then he said, "I immediately thought of you."

And I became a salaried employee with the title of General Manager and Supervisor of Personnel.

It was a pretty good job at that time in my life. I had a salary of $1200 per month and was allowed to drive a company car with a gas allowance. And around Christmas time, Fred would hand out bonuses to the salaried employees, which was him, me, as well as his wife, who kept the books.

My bonus was $1000, which was close to a month's pay.

But I soon found out that being a salaried employee also meant working a ton of hours. Any time that someone did not show up for a shift, guess who got called in to fill the spot? So three or four nights per week I would work someone else's shift and then go back in at 6 AM to do my work. And I guess if I had been single it would not have mattered, but that was not the case. I had a wife and two boys and a baby girl towards the end as well.

In the summer of 1972, Hurricane Agnes came up the Eastern Coast. It was the worst flooding that New York and Pennsylvania had ever seen and it created special problems for us as a contract cleaning company. Thousands of houses were flooded and many of them had carpets that the insurance companies wanted to salvage. So we were hired to pull those carpets out of the houses and try to clean them. Of course, that was a ridiculous idea but we gave it a try nonetheless. Hardly any of those rugs could be salvaged as they were not only filled with river mud but also fuel oil.

In the process, I again tore up my lower back trying to carry a waterlogged piece of carpet on my shoulders. I was out of work for several weeks but finally, I healed up enough to return to work. Thankfully by that time, the idea of trying to clean water and mud-soaked carpeting had been put to rest.

To give you an idea of how many hours our folks were working, I spoke to our rug cleaner and asked him if he was enjoying the overtime pay. His answer was, "Yes the money is good but last night I got off early and when I was coming up the walk towards my house I heard my oldest child yell out, "mommy hurry somebody is coming."

The workload did not let up after I returned to work, though. We kept getting more and more contracts many of them for large offices and trying to find that many good workers was hard. I soon found myself working someone else's shift every night and going back in and doing my supervisory work the next day.

I was becoming frazzled and my wife was becoming unhappy with the fact that I was never home to help her with the kids. I had signed a non-compete clause when I had taken the salaried position, which stated that I could not open my own business within three hundred miles of Olean, New York. I am sure that clause was not enforceable because no substantial amount of money was given in exchange for it but I wasn't going to argue the point.

So I applied for a full-time sales position with Metropolitan Life Insurance Company. I have no idea why I figured it would work out any better than the first time but for some reason I did. Well, Lloyd had moved to Plattsburg, New York to take a regional manager's position with Farmers and Traders.

When Metropolitan contacted him to check my references, he immediately called and asked me if I would consider moving to the North Country as they called it. I talked it over with my wife and we thought we would go up and take a look. It was well over 300 miles from Olean and I figured I could sell some insurance while I built a small cleaning company of my own. So off we went. That was in 1974.

Chapter Eighteen-Global Warming Did Not Exist In Malone, New York

We moved to an old dilapidated house in a little burg called Constable, New York. It was only about 30 miles from Quebec, Canada so you can imagine what the weather might have been like.

We sold our house in Obi, New York for a substantial profit so we could afford to buy this house for cash. With no house payment, it was easier to make ends meet. It was in the summer when we moved up there and I set out to try and start a window-cleaning route. I charged 25 cents per plate of glass per side and many of the local merchants decided that they couldn't clean their windows for that amount of money and I soon had two full days of window cleaning work.

I also went into a couple of the local grocery stores and pitched them on the idea of letting me clean their floors for them using my chemicals and their equipment. Within a short time, I had a pretty good business going and I was selling a fair amount of insurance when I was not doing manual labor.

The window-cleaning route was fairly lucrative at least until winter came to Malone. When it got below freezing I would use straight window washer fluid as my cleaning agent. It worked exceedingly well until the temperature dipped to below 0 degrees. Then even with all that alcohol in the solution, it would gel before it could be squeegeed off the glass. So I set a hard and fast rule that I would not clean windows once the temperature dipped below zero. One winter I did not clean a window for over 30 straight days as the temperature never got above zero.

Even in that bitter cold, my old Ford Van would start. It might complain a little but after a couple of cranks, it would start right up. One day in the middle of that terrible cold a friend of mine called me and asked if I would come and jump his Lincoln as it would not start. It was 35 degrees below zero and the wind was blowing at 35 miles per hour. I am not sure what that made the wind chill factor but I will tell you when I got to where Royal's car was stranded I could not get out of the truck long enough to attach the jumper cables. Instead, I gave him a ride to the bar he owned. He had to return another day to pick up his car.

They used to joke about the seasons in Malone. It was said there were only two seasons in Malone, winter and the fourth of July.

I guess it was sometime in 1976 when I met Rex Thomson. He owned a Laundromat and I stopped in and asked if he would like to hire me to clean his front plate glass windows. He introduced himself and told me he was a "dry Thomson". I guess I must have had a confused look on my face because then he added, "no p".

He hired me to clean his windows, which I did for the next year until he told me one morning that he was thinking of retiring and selling the Laundromat. He asked me if I might be interested since it would go along quite well with the rest of my cleaning business. I asked him how much he wanted for the place and he told me $25,000. I didn't see any way that I could come up with that kind of money and I told him so. After showing me his books so that I could see that it would be a good investment, he offered to carry the loan if I would pay him 10% down.

We struck a deal, I paid him the $2500 and he carried the rest at around $500 per month for 4 years. I wondered why four years and not five but later I found out all to my chagrin. And I also quickly discovered that buying that place was not the great deal that I thought it was. It was supposed to be the kind of Laundromat where it did not require an attendant during the day. It had a bill changer so once it was open it should be okay except for someone stopping by in the middle of the day to clean up and to make sure there were enough quarters in the changer to make it through the rest of the day.

Problem number one was when we discovered that there was not enough water pressure to completely fill the washers since they were on a timer. I called the city to complain and they told me that it was not their problem. Since we were at the highest point we got the least amount of water pressure. So I forked out another thousand dollars to have a heavy-duty pump installed which would pull the water up that hill so that my washers would work. But while that was being done someone had to stay at the Laundromat and fill the washers from buckets. And of course, that was a real pain since it was not only during the initial fill but also during the two rinse cycles. We had 18 washers going at one time. That made it very difficult for any one person to keep up.

Then along came problem number 2. We now had enough water pressure to run the machines but the other side of the building was being remodeled so that it could be turned into a Disco. At first, it seemed to be just a minor inconvenience but then when the place opened it became a much bigger problem. If you are old enough to remember Disco, you also remember that it was extremely loud. And my customers soon started complaining that they were being driven away by that loud pounding music.

I tried reasoning with the owner and then I called the landlord and even discussed the problem with the city police. Eventually, we reached an agreement where the Disco would not start their music until after I closed at 9 p.m. My wife and I even got to the point where we enjoyed stopping by and having a drink while we waited for our late stragglers to finish up.

All in all the Laundromat was an okay deal and might have continued to be so but then I discovered why Rex had only wanted to carry the loan for four years. That was how long the lease on the building was for and the landlord wanted to take over that Laundromat for himself so he refused to renew the lease.

There wasn't another open building that would suit the needs so I had no choice but to close it up and try to sell the equipment for pennies on the dollar.

One of the funniest things that ever happened to me was also associated with that Laundromat. Malone was a small town, not as small as Randolph but small nonetheless. So everyone pretty much knew everyone else especially if you happened to be in business.

As it happened I came to know one of the Town Policemen because his son was on the same little league team as my son. His name was Frank and he was a detective sergeant in the Malone Police Force. So a couple of times a week we would stand behind the batter's cage or on the sidelines and shoot the breeze. I also had a passing acquaintance with one of the State Policemen that was based out of the trooper station in Malone.

I have no idea how long it had been going on but one night after closing up the Laundromat I noticed that a police car was following me. I checked my speedometer and saw that I was well within the legal limit and so I didn't think much else about it. But then for quite some time, the same thing would happen to me. I would close up the Laundromat, get in my car, and check my rearview mirror, and lo and behold there was always a cop car back there. Well, the police force in Malone is not big enough for that kind of coincidence so the next day while I was running my window route, I happened to see Frank and another cop pulled over in front of a car dealership.

I quickly pulled in behind them and got out and approached the car. Frank saw me coming and stepped out to greet me. Wasting no time I said, "All right Frank what in the hell is going on?"

He looked at me kind of strangely and replied. "I have no idea what you mean. What seems to be the problem?"

I said, "Why are your officers following me everywhere I go? Every night there is a cop behind me when I go home."

"It must just be a coincidence," He replied. "The only time your name ever comes up is if we need some help with the team or we need someone to umpire a game."

So I let it slide and the police tails seemed to taper off although I still saw more police cars than I should have.

And then one morning I stopped at the local McDonald's for breakfast. As I was making my way to a seat the State Policeman I mentioned earlier waved me over to sit down with him. I was a little surprised but I joined him just to see what he might have to say.

"Well," He began. "I guess I can tell you now what has been going on." I cocked an eyebrow to let him know I was curious and he continued. "I guess you were wondering why there seemed to be a lot of police cars following you? Well, some folks were using your dryers to dry their marijuana in and we had to make sure you weren't involved in the scheme."

Come to find out they would bring the weed into the Laundromat in pillowcases and put them in the heavy-duty dryers and run it through a couple of cycles to dry it out before processing it.

One of the best things about living in Malone was the fishing was fantastic. There was what we would have called a creek when I was growing up called "The Little Salmon River" that flowed through Constable and the city of Malone. It had a power station on it and a couple of times per day they would let the water out of the dam.

Most of the river was shallow enough so that you could wade out into the middle and fish without the need for a boat. I usually just wore a pair of shorts and a pair of tennis shoes and walked out to the middle where I would cast flies using a spinning rod and a clear plastic bobber that you could fill with water for weight. It was a good alternative to an actual fly rod but it had one drawback. There was always quite a bit of slack line so you had to be quick when a trout would hit your fly.

The Little Salmon had both brown and rainbow trout although none that I ever caught were huge. But it was loads of fun regardless. A lot of times while Lloyd and I were out selling insurance we would take a break for an hour, change into our fishing clothes, and fish.

One memorable day I took my sons, Robert and Shawn fishing with me. I put life jackets on them so I figured they couldn't drown and put them upstream from where I was going to fish. They were fishing and so was I and everyone was having a good time until they let the water out of that dam several miles upstream from where we were. The next thing I knew here comes Shawn floating down the river. I grabbed him by the life jacket and took him to shore just in time to wade back in and do the same for his brother.

My wife and I used to take walks during the winter along the banks of that river and thoroughly enjoyed the beauty of the area.

Chapter Nineteen-Happiness is Owning Your Own Pool Cue

I had always loved playing pool; I just was never any good at it. The first time I ever played was with my brother in a real pool hall in Jamestown, New York. And then I played a few games when I was in the Navy.

But there are very few things to do in Malone, New York for recreation and one of those things was pool. I joined a league that was run by the various bars and because I was playing several times per week I got fairly good.

My fortunes turned for the better one night. I was playing straight pool at the Royal Lounge with a guy I had just met. We were playing for $1 per ball and the game was until someone had reached 50 balls pocketed. In effect, you had to pocket 51 just to make sure you didn't scratch on the last shot. Well, when the game was over he was $5 short on what he owed me and so he gave me his pool cue for the balance.

I had never owned my own stick before. I had always used bar cues and I suspect that my fortunes went according to whether I could find a straight cue or one with a decent tip. It wasn't until years later in Phoenix that I learned about a wonderful little thing that good pool players always carried, called a tip dresser.

So I took his cue and shot a few more games that night with it and I was surprised at how much better control over the cue ball I had with that stick. It wasn't perfectly straight but I soon learned that if you put one of the plastic diamonds that were in the handle straight up then the bend did not matter much.

With that cue, I was beginning to get pretty good. Shortly after that, I heard about a tournament that was being run in every bar in town and some that were on the outskirts of town.

All it cost you to get into a weekly tournament was the cost of the quarters for the table. The tables at that time were a dollar and each match was the best two out of three so it was pretty cheap entertainment. There was no cash prize for the winner of the weekly tournament. It just allowed you to play off against all the other weekly winners at the end of the tournament.

That winner got a whopping $5,000.

Well, I wasn't so vain as to think I had any chance of winning that money but I loved the idea of playing the best players in the area.

They had some strange rules that I was not used to and it cost me a few games before I caught on to how some of the people played. One was the three-foul rule. If you committed three fouls in any one game you lost that game. A foul was failing to hit your ball before you hit another, failing to take at least one ball or the cue ball to the rail, moving a ball with your hands or any part of your clothing or body, or scratching the cue ball. If you committed a foul shooting at the eight ball you automatically lost.

Some of the players loved to win by fouling out their opponents. To me, that was dirty pool but it was part of the rules so you had to watch out for it. I remember playing with one guy that refused to make a ball until all his balls were in front of the pockets. He would just roll his balls toward the pockets, leaving his opponent blocked behind one or more of his balls. If you did not realize what he was doing you were sitting on the sidelines watching the other players rack the balls.

Well, he got me one time playing that way but the next time I played the same game against him. Of course, I made it look more like I was trying to make my balls than he did but the result was the same. He fouled out both games he played me and when it was over came over and said. "You wanted me pretty badly, didn't you?"

Some of the tournaments took place on Sunday afternoons since most people did not have to work then and church services were over before the tournaments started. I remember one Sunday when I started at the Royal Lounge early in the afternoon. I won my first match and drew a woman to play against in the second. I don't think she tried to play dirty; she was just so terrible that I ended up always behind her balls and I fouled out both games.

Since I was out of that tournament early enough I decided to drive to another bar across town and try my hand there. As I walked into the bar to sign up I announced fairly loudly that I hoped I drew AJ Riley (perhaps the best pool player in Malone) in the first round so I could lose and go home.

A few minutes later the pairings were announced and sure enough, I was scheduled to play my first match against AJ. He broke and ran all but one ball but left himself a tough bank shot, which just barely missed going in. I picked up my cue and ran the table. I had the break in the second game and ran the table without giving him a shot.

I figured that I might have a chance after that. My second opponent was not nearly as good as AJ but in my first game, I scratched on the eight ball giving him that game. I won the next two games and never lost another game that afternoon. So now I was a weekly winner entitled to play in the finals a few weeks down the road.

I also won another weekly tournament at another bar later in the same week, but you could only play for one bar so I had to concede that to the second-place winner.

When the finals came along I blew it. I had a fairly easy straight-in shot at the eight ball in the first game but the cue ball was against the rail. I knew very little about playing English except for stop-and-go. I tried to put a little left-hand English on the cue to keep it out of the pocket but it went the exact opposite way of what I thought it should and I scratched. I was so shaken up by that mishap that I fouled out my second game. My prize was $25.

After moving to Phoenix, I played a friendly game of pool about once a week but never played for money again.

Chapter Twenty-The Arizona Kid and the Pirates of Medlock Drive

They called him the Arizona Kid and he looked the part from the Stetson hat that sat atop his head to the western buckle on his belt to the cowboy boots he wore on his feet. He was not a particularly large man although a synonym for large was used when my neighbor's wife described him as being bigger, badder, and better than her husband Donnie. I suppose she could have been referring to a particular part of his anatomy because when she said it she was preparing to leave her husband and begin living with Dan.

Donnie was a friend of mine and so I had severe doubts that I would become anything more than a casual acquaintance with Phyllis's new lover. But Phyllis was also a friend of my wife so it was bound that our paths would cross more than occasionally. Add to that the fact that Dan was also a pool player that frequented the same bars that I did and you had the recipe for more than a casual relationship.

He was highly competitive and so was I so our games of pool got quite intense. And as the competition grew so did our friendship. I learned he was going to college in Malone but would be returning to Phoenix after his next semester. He said that his brother was starting an electronics business and that Dan was going back to run it for him.

The lease on my Laundromat was due to expire shortly after Dan left and so when he asked if I would be interested in working for him in Phoenix it did not take much arm bending to get me to agree. I told him that I would join him in the endeavor if he could pay me $25,000 per year. When he replied that he was thinking more along the lines of $500 a week (I could do that math in my head) I made plans to sell what we had in Malone and move what was left to Phoenix.

Before selling everything we owned I made a trip by myself to Phoenix. The trip across the country took me five days. I could have made it in three but when I gassed up in Missouri I did not realize that the gasoline was laced with ethanol. It cleaned out my fuel system but clogged my fuel filter and caused my fuel pump to self-destruct.

So I found myself stuck in a little town in New Mexico called Gallop, for two days while they ordered another fuel pump and installed it.

I finally reached Phoenix. Dan had given me his address but I was completely lost in a city that size. When it became obvious to me that I had probably passed the street he lived on I stopped at a convenience store and used a payphone to call him.

He acted surprised to receive my call which I could not understand since he had been the one that had suggested I come to Phoenix to work with him, to begin with. However, once he heard where I was he did drive down to meet me and allow me to follow him back to his place.

Then the shock set in when he told me he had never expected me to come to Phoenix, to begin with. I was pissed at that point having driven 2500 miles for a job that now sounded like it didn't exist. I asked him why he had asked me to work for him in the first place. He replied that he didn't think I would take him seriously and now that I was there he didn't think that I could do the job in any event.

Well, hell, I didn't even know what the job entailed but I figured that I had never failed at any other job in my life so why couldn't I do this one? So I asked him to explain what this mystery job was all about.

It turned out that he was manufacturing decoders for a TV service called "On TV". What that amounted to was that the local UHF television station, Channel 15 stopped normal broadcasting at 10 pm and began broadcasting soft porn for which they charged a subscription fee. Dan was manufacturing "black boxes" that would down-convert the signal and decode it so that it could be watched without paying the subscription. He sold those units for $160 apiece. He needed someone to build and test those units for him as he had too many customers to do all of the work himself.

Perhaps had I known of what he was doing before I drove 2500 miles I might not have been so eager to show him that I could do the work. But, once I was already there I figured I had little choice so I insisted that he allow me to at least try to do what needed to be done.

So we drove down to one of the worst sections of the City where his shop was located. He grabbed a few of those units that had not yet been tested and we took them back to his house. He showed me how to adjust the four spin wheels on the circuit board so that all the squiggly lines on the TV screen would straighten out. He used an oscilloscope and took a long time testing each pin of several of the IC chips before finally getting the unit to work.

So he said, "Now you see why you can't do the job?"

I said, "No, give me one."

I hooked it up to the Television as I had watched him do and without the benefit of the oscilloscope, I started turning knobs until the picture was as clear as his had been. He allowed me to keep working for an hour or so and finally, I came to a unit that simply would not tune. So I told him that there was something wrong with the unit. He said, "No there isn't, I told you that you couldn't do it."

"Okay, then smart ass I said, you do this one." He fiddled with it for the longest time and then he got a shit-eating grin on his face as he looked at me and said. "You were right, it is a bad unit."

So after spending that first night bickering back and forth he finally agreed that since I was already there he would agree to let me work with him.

I soon learned that the biggest problem he was having with those decoders was the person that was supplying the parts for him. It seems he was in partnership with a man named Richard. Richard owned a parts store and he supplied the parts and Dan supplied the labor and expertise and they split the profits. Well, Richard wanted to maximize his investment so he gave us second-hand parts that had been salvaged from other projects. It was no surprise that a lot of them did not work properly.

I finally suggested to Dan that we build a couple of sample units with IC sockets instead of the chips being hard-soldered to the board so that we could test each IC before it was permanently installed. It did add some labor time but in the long run, it saved a good deal of aggravation. Instead of solder-wicking bad ICs out of the boards, we could just pull them out of the sockets and set them aside to be returned to Richard for replacements.

At some point, the quality of the parts got so bad that I suggested to Dan that we give up on the great Richard experiment and buy our own parts from a reputable parts house. He told me that he could not afford to do that, as the parts for each unit would cost $80 if he had to buy them new.

Again we had to argue and bicker but I finally convinced him that we could each put in $1000, which would buy enough parts for 25 units. When we sold them we could put the profit back into a run of 50 and keep doing that until we had enough capital to make a run of 100 units.

That worked exceptionally well. We soon had quality parts that very seldom ever failed and we had happy customers who came back week after week for more products. Eventually, Dan got so comfortable with my skills that he decided to take me on as a full partner with him supplying the parts and I supplied the labor. So every week we would make and test 100 units and sell them for cash.

One of our buyers was an African American man by the name of Henry. For some time, he would buy 100 units every week himself and resell them. I would go with Dan when he delivered the products and

Henry would pay him in cash. He would hand Dan 16000 dollars in hundred dollar bills. Dan would take 8000 dollars and put it in his left shirt pocket for parts money, hand me 4000 for my share, and put the other 4000 in his right shirt pocket.

One day after making that delivery Dan stopped to buy a pack of cigarettes from a Circle K store. I stayed in the truck while he went in and waited for him. I could see him through the windows talking and smiling with a young female clerk and finally, he made his purchase and came back out. As he got into the truck he said, "That was easy."

"I said what was easy?" He said, "I got a date with that girl for Friday night." He was all happy and proud of himself until I asked the question of the hour.

"Was that before or after you tried to buy a pack of cigarettes with 8000 dollars?"

We had a great business going for a little while. In fact, every member of my family had a part in producing those units. Some were able to stuff boards and solder others put the boxes together and assembled the units. As time went on we needed more help than what the six of us could handle and so we hired a couple of neighbor kids that went to school with my oldest son. Their names were Dave and John and they were twins. They were always cracking jokes and they kept us in stitches most of the time.

Well, one morning Dan called me and told me that Henry had a new customer that was going to be coming by Henry's place and picking up some units and Dan needed to know who this guy was. So he asked me to take a drive-by and see if I could get a look at this person. I thought that it was strange but not having as much of a suspicious mind as I do today I did as I was asked.

I didn't see anything out of the ordinary and so I drove back home. About an hour later Dan called me again with this message. "I wouldn't take it too seriously but I also wouldn't take it too lightly. Henry was just arrested and taken down to the local police station."

Well, let me tell you I did take it very seriously. Within an hour, every box, IC, capacitor, resistor, and anything else associated with the manufacture of On TV units was cleaned out of that little shed in the backyard. Even the cracks in the floorboards had been vacuumed and the resistor leads picked up. Each member of our crew was called and told not to come back to work until we let them know.

That night the twins were eating dinner and watching the news with their mother when the story of the On TV bust came on. The newscaster said, "Today Henry _ _ _ _ _ _ was arrested, not for having stolen equipment but for having equipment that steals." And they showed pictures of about 100 of our units.

John looked at the screen with surprise and started to say "Those look just like the units that" he left the rest unsaid as he saw his mother staring at him with suspense in her eyes.

Although Henry did continue to buy product from us, business never did get back to the same level as before his arrest.

We still made a few units and sold them to small dealers but finally, we switched to making units for picking up HBO over-the-air signals. This lasted only for a short time and then Dan stopped bringing parts to the house. I would call and Phyllis would always tell me that Dan was sleeping and she refused to wake him up. At some point, I began to run low on money and I knew that I would have to do something else. And then I found out why Dan was always sleeping during the day. It seems he had developed the habit of snorting white powder up his nose at night making it impossible for him to sleep.

Out of desperation, I finally struck a deal with Henry to manufacture a few On TV units and a few HBO units for him. He would supply the parts and I would charge him labor at a set rate per unit. This worked fine for a short time but then Henry decided he wanted a bigger piece of the pie so he asked me to cut my rate which I did the first time. But soon he wanted it cut again and I knew that I would be working for nothing shortly so I refused.

He tried reasoning with me from a position of strength. "A little bit of something is better than a lot of nothing," He argued.

"My response was 100% of nothing is still nothing."

He stormed out of the shop and I didn't hear from him for a few days. Then he called and started to threaten me. "I could have turned you in when I was busted and I still can if we can't work something out."

My response. "Don't threaten me, Henry. I do very bad things when I feel threatened."

And the threats went back and forth for a little while longer.

I still sold a few units here and there and finally, Henry came back and asked me to start building his product for him again. I guess he figured out that it was better to have product that worked at a slightly higher price than product that was cheaper but didn't perform.

In the meantime, we purchased our own home on Medlock Dr. in Phoenix. The house had a grandmother's addition that we turned into a workshop. We were now selling not only to Henry but also to a man named Sam from Scottsdale as well.

Sam sold some of his product to a legitimate broadcaster from Guadalajara, Mexico. And through him, I met a man from Albuquerque, New Mexico that sold to a broadcaster in Panama City, Panama.

The pirate side of the business had almost died out because complete units were coming into the country from Japan for less than what it cost me for parts to build the electronics alone. So I struck up a deal with the broadcaster in Panama to sell him the right to manufacture the power supplies and down converters to use for his station. Rene lived in McLean, Virginia and he had me fly out to his home to finalize the deal.

I didn't get a whole lot of money out of the deal but I did get a trip to Panama City to work with his engineering staff.

I arrived in the early autumn of 1989. The chief engineer's name was Carlos Brown although everyone called him Charley Brown. I never did think he looked like anything out of a Peanut cartoon. I spent a week down there trying to get my down converters to work well with their system and I never was overly successful. I rode around with Charley Brown and visited some of their receivers and tried different things. One day we stopped at a large house with a guarded gate and I was told to stay in the truck while Charley went in to check on some satellite equipment. I was amazed to see so many armed soldiers walking around with weapons at the ready.

There was not a lot of good that I will say about that trip, the food was absolutely terrible. I ate almost raw chicken and calamari that tasted like rubber. But the absolute worst part of that trip was the airplanes that I rode on the way home.

From Panama to Mexico City I flew Lacsa, the official airline of Costa Rico. The take-off was not too bad but then we set down in Guatemala for a three-hour layover. When he hit the runway the plane bounced back into the air and then came down hard and bounced again. Everyone deplaned and went into the terminal to wait for the plane to be serviced.

We finally got back on board and the pilot started to accelerate down the runway but just before takeoff he hit the brakes and the plane skidded sideways off of the runway. I was sitting just behind the wing and I looked down and noticed that he had never put his flaps down. He must have realized that at the last possible second. If he had got that plane airborne it would not have stayed in the air long.

So back to the terminal, we went supposedly to fix a mechanical difficulty. Finally, we did take off for Mexico City. Again when we landed he put it down so hard that we bounced back up in the air and again a second time.

I spent the night in Mexico City and the next day changed planes. This time, the airline was Mexicana and I rode that until we got to Guadalajara. This pilot was a little better than the last one but not by enough that I wanted to ride with him ever again. I had some business to conduct with the broadcaster in Guadalajara and so I spent the morning and early afternoon with him. I had my flight booked on Mexicana from Guadalajara to Los Angeles later that afternoon. But when we concluded our business early and I had a couple of hours before my flight was due to board I went to the Continental counter and asked how much it would cost me to switch my flight to them. It was the best $25 I ever spent.

I am truly amazed that there are no more very serious accidents on those airlines. Unless I got the only two incompetent pilots on those two airlines they should be losing planes right and left.

As my plane lifted off from Los Angeles to Phoenix, I looked out the window to one of the most glorious scenes I had ever seen. The woman sitting beside me had her head in her hands and her eyes tightly shut. I said, "Pardon me ma'am but you are missing a truly beautiful view."

She didn't even raise her head. She just said, "You fly your way and I'll fly mine."

I wasn't insulted. I just figured she had come in on Mexicana.

On a side note to the trip to Panama. I had not been home very long when the United States invaded that country. I heard that Carlos Brown was shot in that invasion although I do not believe fatally. It seems he was attending a party at Noriega's Palace the night of the invasion. I believe that was the same building that he visited when I was with him and he told me to stay in the vehicle.

I was effectively out of the black box business at that point and I needed a job. So I applied to Radio Shack and was hired as a sales associate. It was an extremely easy job except for the fact that the only way to make any serious money was to talk people into buying vastly overpriced electronics. Most of their customers came in looking for resistors or capacitors for small electronic projects they might be building and unless you could up-sell them something you weren't going to make much commission.

The store manager's name was Holly and she was a crotchety old woman. If even the slightest thing went wrong during a shift she would fly into a rage so when the schedule came out I was always happiest if I was not scheduled to work with her.

Once in a while though it was fun to compete with her. I remember one Saturday when we had a special on videotape. She bet me a soda that she could sell more videotape than I could. I figured that on her best day she didn't stand a chance in that department. She would stand behind the counter and wait until a customer had found what he or she was looking for and then on check out she would try to hit them up for a pack or two of tape.

I, on the other hand, followed every customer that came in the door trying to help them find the resistor, capacitor, or battery that they were there to get. And then on the way back to the counter, I would start my spiel. "By the way, as long as you are here, you might as well take advantage of the most fantastic offer on genuine Memorex videotape you will ever see. Buy a five-pack and save big bucks. Is it live or is it Memorex?"

When the shift was over I had sold 27 5-packs of tape while Holly had sold 9. I probably would have stayed with the company for quite some time but one day Holly had me working on changing light bulbs in the ceiling. I felt something snap in my back and my entire right side went numb. I managed to get down without falling but I couldn't work anymore that day. And the next day I was in so much pain that I could not go back in.

Finally, after about two weeks I went to a doctor. A disc in my back had finally given all it was going to give. I never went back to work at Radio Shack. I had to wait for months to get that disc removed and by the time they did take it out, it had exploded.

I was taking two Vicodin and then two hours later two Percosette capsules and even then they hardly dulled the pain. Twice while I was waiting for surgery I had to go in to get an injection for pain. I have no idea how many brain cells I burned during that time but I do know I had no short-term memory left.

I also had three short stints trying to be a car salesman. None of them lasted very long. I think the first time I tried to sell cars was for Dodge City in Phoenix. That was by far the worst experience. If I thought Holly was bad as a manager, those guys in the tower were 10 times worse. Then I sold Toyota for a while. The best part of that experience was that I met a guy by the name of Dave Foster. He was a good car salesman and I learned a lot from him.

I remember one day when a customer came on the lot and told Dave he could get the exact car down the street for 2500 dollars less than we were asking. Dave said to him, 2500 dollars, less, why didn't you buy it?"

The customer looked all flustered and then said, "They didn't have any."

Dave chuckled and said, "I will sell you anything we don't have for 2500 dollars less too."

In our downtime, which was far too often we use to build each other up with motivational quotes. They would go something like this. Dave would say, "You know around every silver lining there is a deep dark cloud."

I would reply, "It is always darkest just before it goes totally black."

And then Dave would pop something like, "A wet bird never flies at night."

Even though I didn't last in that job very long I stayed friends with Dave until I left Phoenix in 1997. We would get together every once in a while and go out into the desert and shoot our .357 handguns at tin cans and have a great time.

And my wife and I would get together with Dave and his wife and go to one of the Indian casinos every once in a while. To hear them tell it they must have been the luckiest gamblers alive. They always seemed to win a ton of money at the slots. I often wondered though if they were counting how much they fed into the one-armed bandits.

I know for a fact that only once in my life did I walk out of a casino with more money than I walked in. That happened in a little Indian casino in Prescott, Arizona. I was playing the quarter slots and my wife was playing nickel slots. I had dropped $80 and walked over to Janice and told her I thought it was time to go. She replied that she had a whole bucket of nickels and she wanted to play them out. So I said, "Give me some. I am an expert at losing money in slot machines."

I moved down two machines from where my wife was sitting and put in one nickel. I hit two cherries, which I think paid 4 nickels. I put in another and fit three bars which paid ten. So I thought why not and fed three nickels into the machine? Well, the bells started ringing and the lights started flashing and soon an attendant came over to my machine. I had hit a progressive jackpot that paid $375. I got my chit and walked back to my wife and said, "I don't care how many nickels you have left. For once, I want to leave a winner."

Chapter Twenty-One Saudi Arabia Might Be a Dry Country but its Citizens Are Not

Although trying to sell microwave antennas in the United States became increasingly difficult people were still buying them in other parts of the world. In fact, the people of Saudi Arabia were buying them in huge quantities. Some of the princes of that country were broadcasting CNN to the people in their realms. While that was a clear violation of that country's standards nothing was done since it was the royalty that was doing it. And so they would buy our microwave antennas and resell them to those that wanted to watch the Western news.

At some point, though they needed to scramble their signal and they did this by introducing noise into the outer band of the broadcast. Well, I had been making filters to cut out just that type of interference and selling them to the country of Haiti so I figured I could manage to come up with something to work on their scrambled signal as well. But not having anyone in that country that knew anything about what they were doing or being able to relay what they were seeing to me, I had no choice. If I wanted to continue to sell microwave units over there I would have to go there to solve the problem.

I had met a man by the name of Joe who was also working on a deal to sell satellite antennas in Saudi Arabia and so we got together and found one of the princes to sponsor our entry into the country. There is no such thing as a quick trip in and out of the country. The minimum stay is 8 days and, believe me, those become the longest 8 days of your life.

Before we could even book a flight we had to sign a statement saying that we agreed to be beheaded if they found drugs or alcohol in our possession.

When we got there and went through their customs one of the questions they asked was are you carrying any sweets. I thought that was a strange question and so I asked them to repeat it. Sure enough, that was what they were asking about candy, particularly chocolates that might contain alcohol like chocolate cordials.

We spent our days either working on my filter or Joe's satellite business. One day we had an appointment with another of the thousands of princes that live in that country. As we walked through his courtyard we saw a flashing Budweiser sign and in the window next to the entryway was a handwritten sign that said, "If you drive me to drink, I will buy the gas." Of course, at about a dime a gallon that would have been a good deal for him.

We were shocked to see that the women dressed from the top of their heads to the tops of their shoes in long black robes and with black face coverings. It was every bit as hot there as it was in Arizona and we thought that was cruel and unusual punishment for them, women. The men, on the other hand, wore pure white robes. We asked one husband why he wore white robes. "Well, white is very cool," He replied. "Then why do you force your women to wear black?" We asked.

If looks could have killed we would not have made it out of there alive.

When the eight days were over and we were on the plane leaving Riyadh, the drink cart came out while the plane was barely off the runway. The flight attendant was handing out alcoholic bottles left and right and every single passenger was gladly accepting them. The guy I was with reached over and took two before the flight attendant could hand them to him. She chastised him and told him he could have all he wanted but not to reach for it himself. I said, "Joe you don't even drink."

"No!" He exclaimed. But nobody is going to tell me that I can't."

Our plane landed in Frankfurt, Germany and we spent the night in a hotel there. The following morning we went to the airport around 6 am to board our flight to Houston, Texas. Every 50 feet or so everyone was stopped and asked security questions. They went something like this. "Did you pack your own luggage before you left the hotel? Has your luggage been within your sight ever since you left your hotel? Has anyone tried to give you anything to take on board the airplane for them? Where did you stay in Saudi Arabia? What was the purpose of your visit to Saudi Arabia?"

This was repeated at least 6 times before we got to the gate and once more before we could go through the gate to our plane. The last question I was asked was, "And if you should return to Saudi Arabia,"

I didn't wait for him to finish. I simply emphatically declared, "Not in this lifetime."

Chapter Twenty-Two-More Black Boxes

At some point, I met another Dave, this time, Dave Porter. He lived in a trailer park in Apache Junction, Arizona and he made his living selling cable equipment. I had never even considered doing that although I had certainly worked around the fringes of that business for many years. Well, I needed something to make some money so I got a few descramblers from him and found out that they worked very well. All you needed was basic cable, a converter box that you could buy at Radio Shack, and one of these descramblers and you could watch anything that was on including pay-per-view.

Most people were selling the things for around 200 dollars and the cost of the descramblers was 70 or 80 dollars depending on how many you bought.

After checking the thing out, I figured that I could manufacture them and save some money so I had a circuit board made locally and began building my own. First I tried to sell strictly to distributors so that I would have a level of protection between the law and me. But there just were not that many people that wanted to resell the equipment. Even though I was making the boxes at a lower cost than buying them through the electronics magazines, I had to make a profit or it didn't make sense.

So eventually, I started selling directly to customers. I would put a little ad in one of the adult magazines that were sold all over Phoenix and people would call me up to come to hook the thing up for them. I charged 175 dollars per unit.

It worked pretty well for a while. But then the word came down that there was a major bust about to take place. So I tried to hide my business a little more than usual. I refused to deliver them anymore but if they wanted to come to my house I would sell them. But I had a lot of those ads floating out there and the phone rang continually.

On top of that, I was waiting for back surgery at that time and my mind was not working as clearly as it should be. Some of the calls were so obvious that even with my hazy brain I could deflect them. They would go something like this. "I will buy the cable descrambler from you if you bring it to my house and deliver it." "Sorry, I can't do that."

"Then you are going to lose a lot of money. You realize that don't you?"

The harder they would push, the surer I was that they were working for the cable company.

But as with all disorganized crime, I slipped up. I allowed three guys to come into my house at the same time and buy a descrambler. I didn't think much about it although I should have recognized it for what it was when he asked if he should disconnect the unit if a technician had to be called out. I should have told him that if he was planning on using the unit for illegal purposes I couldn't sell it to him but I guess my brain was too addled to figure that out.

Well, I finally had my back surgery and was in the recovery stage, doing physical therapy, and was almost back on my feet when one day I heard a knock on the door. I went to answer it with a cable box in my hand and the guy on the other side handed me a subpoena and told me that I was ordered to appear in court on such and such a date and that I would have to stop by the police station for fingerprints and photographs before that time.

I was just one of over thirty people that they caught in those stings. I hired a lawyer that specialized in criminal law hoping that he would find a way to get me clear of the charges. But alas that was not to be.

Finally, the District Attorney offered us a plea bargain reducing the charges from a Class One Felony to a Class Two Misdemeanor and I accepted to avoid a permanent record. I was supposed to receive a 2500-dollar fine, one hundred hours of community service, and one year of unsupervised probation.

Unfortunately, I got a judge that was a hard ass. He insisted that the deal was too lenient for a dangerous criminal such as me and so he changed the probation to supervised. That meant that I would be subject to weekly visits by my probation officer and random alcohol and drug tests. Another stipulation was that I was not to have any weapons in my possession.

Of course, I owned a high-powered rifle, a shotgun, and a .357 magnum revolver. So to get around that stipulation, I turned them over to one of my sons for safekeeping.

Community service became a slight problem since I was still recovering from my back operation. Typically I would have been assigned to some form of manual labor, picking up trash along the highways or cleaning toilets in a public building. But I had a doctor's note excusing me from any form of physical labor. Next, my probation officer tried to get me involved in helping out in the office of a local church but they refused my help. The only people they used for community service were drunk driving offenders. I have no idea why that rule was in place.

There isn't a whole lot that could be said for this heading. This was what I finally ended up doing for my community service and I could do it from my own home. I answered the phone for a missing pet line called "Missing Mutts".

If someone had lost a pet, they would call our hotline and report it along with a description and general area where it was lost. I would take that information down so that if someone found that animal they could also report it to us and I could call the owner back.

My daughter thought hearing me answer our phone, "missing mutts, how can I help you today?" was hilarious and so I had to include this in my book.

I was required to work at this venture for 20 hours per week but I put in closer to 25 so my community service ended in about a month. And as soon as my community service ended so did the visitations by my parole officer.

Chapter Twenty-Three-A Kiosk Inside Wal-Mart

In the late fall of 1995, I was again looking for something to do to make money to support my family. I would get the Sunday paper and go through all the ads, starting with the sales ads. I had agreed with my wife that if I ever again tried selling cars, she could shoot me and she had readily agreed to the deal so I discounted anything having to do with automobiles.

I came across a little tiny ad that gave little information other than it involved retail sales and asked for applicants to fax in a resume.

I knew that they were desperate because the ink could not have dried on the other end of the line before my phone began to ring. I was told that the job involved selling wireless telephones to customers within retail establishments.

I didn't have anything else to do so I agreed to an interview in a little office on Greenway road, almost to the city of Scottsdale.

This outfit was not much to instill confidence because when you entered the office there was only one desk and two chairs in the main room. The owner I discovered had his own tiny office off to one side. Phone boxes were stacked everywhere where there was room for them and if more than two people needed to sit down, the extra people would have to sit on a pile of phone boxes.

The interview was fairly short. A young man by the name of Tim Denman interviewed me. He asked me a few questions about the jobs that I had worked at and then asked me how I felt about standing for long hours inside a kiosk in Walmart and greeting people as they walked by to get them to buy a phone.

The job paid $4 per hour plus a commission of $25 per phone sale and a little extra for each dollar of accessories sold. I figured I might be able to sell two phones per day if I was lucky. I wasn't going to get rich doing it but I wasn't going to get rich sitting at home either so I agreed to give it a try.

I was supposed to have two full days of training but that didn't happen. Denman took me to a kiosk in Mesa on a Sunday morning and sold one phone. Then he looked at me and said, stay here and see what you can do. I would like to be able to give you the keys but I don't know where I put them and then left. So I stood there reading whatever literature I could find about cellular telephones for the rest of the day. I quickly discovered that if I was going to be successful at this job it was not going to be because of an extensive training program.

Somehow I managed to sell 10 phones in my first two weeks and 44 phones in December. A funny thing also happened while I was there. I learned that some store managers would allow the sales reps to use the PA system to try and attract customers to their booth locations. I had never spoken on a PA system before but thought it couldn't be that hard and so I stepped up to the telephone they used and began to speak. "Attention K-Mart shoppers I began. I went through the entire spiel before the store manager was in my face explaining that I was not in K-Mart. That set my announcement experiment back just a little. What I did do was sell a goodly amount of accessories. That was a carryover from working at Radio Shack and having it drummed into my head that no customer should ever leave the store without something more than they came in to buy.

Early in January, we had a meeting and I made the mistake of listening to some of the old-timers (those that had been there the previous January) tell me that you could not sell phones in January.

That was because everyone had spent all their money on Christmas and their credit cards were maxed out.

And because I believed them, I didn't sell very many phones in January. I sold exactly 30 phones that month. I figured that shortly someone would come by and fire me and so when the owner showed up one day I figured that this new career had come to an end. But instead of firing me, he commended me for selling the second most dollar amount of accessories and I learned that I was number 3 in phone sales for the month.

I should have known better than to listen to someone complain about what I could or could not do in sales. I remember one car manager telling us once that salesmen are always okay until someone tells them the truth. He went on to relate how he had walked out on the front lines of a car dealership he had just taken over and approached one of the salespeople and asked him how it was going. The man looked back at him with disdain on his face and said. "It is Tuesday and Tuesdays always suck." The manager then asked him how long he had been with the company. The man replied, "I started last Wednesday."

In February, I got back up to 45 phones, and a new store opened in North Phoenix. When I had taken the job Denman had told me that if something opened closer to my home I could transfer to that store. And so when I heard about this new store opening I called him and told him that I wanted to transfer. He immediately said no, that he had a lot of people that wanted that store and they had been with the company longer.

Well, that was not the understanding that I had been led to believe would happen and so I gave him my two weeks' notice.

I learned later that he had told one of the owners why I was quitting and they insisted that he live up to the word he had given me when I was hired. I never did get along well with Tim after that. I wondered if he did not find me threatening since I was a lot older and had a ton more experience as a manager than he did. Anyway, Tim gave me the new store but he told me that he expected great things from the store (he did not say he expected great things from me). So I replied that I guaranteed him that I would be the agent of the year. He looked at me and just laughed. He did not even try to hide his derision.

I also learned at that time that there was a bonus system in place for top sales producers. It seems that someone had challenged Barry Miller one of the owners to offer a bonus of 1000 dollars if someone could sell 100 phones in any calendar month.

His response was sure, I will make that deal because no one could ever sell 100 phones in a month from a kiosk inside Walmart.

I started in my new store on the first of March and I sold 5 phones the first day and then four more the second day. I thought I was doing fantastic until I heard that another salesperson was selling a lot more phones than I was. Her name was Kathy and she worked at one of the highest-volume stores but it was also one of the poorest for credit approval.

I remember one night I was working late and the phone rang. I answered it and it was Kathy. She said, "I knew you would be working late and I just have to vent to someone. I just ran my 30th application today without one approval."

When March ended she had sold 153 phones becoming the first person to ever sell over 100 phones in one month. I was the second with 112 phones sold and 2600 dollars worth of accessories. In April, I again sold 112 phones and another 2500 dollars worth of accessories. I thought that a 1000 dollar bonus would be mine every month. But nothing is that easy. I did get it twice more that year. In July, I sold exactly 100 phones. It was looking doubtful as late as 7 PM on the 31st. I was sitting at exactly 98 phones and I was running out of friends and relatives to call begging them to come in and buy one.

Denman called me and asked where I was and kind of laughed when I told him. "Too bad I guess we won't be paying any 1000-dollar bonus this month." 7 was typically closing time but the store did not close until 9 so I still had a chance. But I also had an ace in the hole. I had already run my credit and I was approved for two lines. I told that to Denman later and he said, "You really wouldn't have bought two phones just to get that bonus would you?" I said, "Hell, yes, I would have but I didn't need to. I sold two phones just before 9 that night."

In May Cellular One changed its promotion to something totally inane. They were offering 20 extra minutes of off-peak airtime. But there was a caveat, you couldn't use that off-peak airtime until you had exhausted the minutes that came with your plan. I thought that was the most stupid thing I had ever heard and so I refused to mention the promotion to the customers. And one night when I was fed up, I made a huge mistake. When I called in to give my numbers I left the following message. "Somebody should tell Cell One that their promotion sucks."

The next day Tim showed up at my kiosk and told me never to do that again. It had pissed off one of the owners because he believed that any promotion was better than no promotion and the carriers didn't have to offer a promotion.

Well, a few months later we had a company party. When I walked in the door I saw Barry Miller (the owner) standing and talking with a group of people. I walked straight up to him and said, "Am I forgiven yet, Barry? He replied, "It is easy to forgive someone that sells a lot of phones for me."

And in December I sold 114 phones. There was also a 1000 bonus for the most phones sold in a calendar year, which I also received. I wouldn't have gotten that bonus but they made Kathy a manager in August of that year making her ineligible for the bonus.

Most of my success in that or any other store I ever worked in was because of learning to say Wal-Mart on the PA system. They allowed me to make announcements three times per hour and I religiously did that.

I made announcements faithfully every 20 minutes and I added one extra announcement the hour before lunch and the hour before the store closed. That was because I had found out that people responded well to the threat that an offer would end in 15 minutes. In sales, there are two main reasons that people will impulse buy. Greed and the fear of loss. So at quarter till 2 in the afternoon, I would get on the pa system and announce, "The cellular one booth in the center aisle will close in 15 minutes. However, there is still time to get a free cellular telephone with the best rate plan in Arizona. Don't miss out on this fantastic offer. It will end in 15 minutes." And then at 6:45 in the evening I would repeat that announcement. Frequently I would sell more phones in those two hours than the rest of the day put together.

Today, many years later I have to laugh when I hear Mike Lyndell say that you need to buy his slippers because once they are gone they are gone. He obviously knows about the fear of loss theory.

I was always trying to come up with new and better announcements and even started writing a few poems to say over the loudspeaker. One day I talked my daughter into doing a tape with me. It was a take-off of Romeo and Juliet and it went something like this. She would say, "Romeo, Romeo where for have you been Romeo." I would reply, "Juliet my light the traffic is murder out there, and where douth one find a pay phone on the throughway?" "Romeo have you not heard that cellular service from cellular one is truly affordable and the phone is free."

Well, I played that over the intercom and the store manager came back a few minutes later and said, "Wayne you have outdone yourself this time. We always enjoy your announcement but this one has my cashiers laughing so hard they can't get any work done."

About halfway through the following year, they asked for volunteers to go to Tulsa, Oklahoma to help roll out that area as a new market. They agreed to pay double the commission to anyone that would agree to help in that regard. I thought it would be a great opportunity to make a little extra money so I signed on for two weeks.

Our best rate plan with Cellular One, in Phoenix, was $30 for 30 minutes of airtime. Ridiculous as it may seem I would sell that by saying, "a lot of airtime for that low amount of money."

I think two other salespeople went with me along with our sales manager Tim Denman. Imagine my surprise when I got there and went through a four-hour training course to find that they were giving 200 minutes for $30. Well, I practically skipped for joy.

Tulsa like Phoenix was a combination market, meaning it had both Wal-Marts and grocery stores where we had kiosks. In Phoenix, nobody wanted to work the grocery stores because they were dirty and the class of people coming in were poor credit at best. It soon became common knowledge that you could not sell phones out of grocery stores.

On my first day in Tulsa, I was assigned to work at a Walmart and because of my enthusiasm for the rate plans, I sold 11 phones. That night at dinner the market manager, Garrett Roof approached me. After congratulating me on a fantastic day, he asked me if I would consider working at a grocery store the next day. I informed him that I was there to help in whatever capacity he needed so sure.

While I was not quite as successful, I did sell nine phones out of a Reasor's grocery store. In fact, I averaged six phones per day for my first 10 days in the market alternating between Wal-Marts and Reasor's. And that included a couple of days when I conducted training for new hires.

They were rapidly expanding the market and when my two weeks were up they asked me to stay on for another two.

But finally, it was time to leave and Garrett approached me and asked if I would be willing to stay on in the market. I told him not as a salesman but if he wanted me there as a manager I would consider it.

He forwarded the request to the owners and got approval, so we packed up the truck and moved to Mannford.

Chapter Twenty Four-I Don't Own a Dog Named Toto and I Don't Live in Kansas

My wife came out and found us a place to live. It was a doublewide trailer on the outskirts of the thriving metropolis of Mannford, Oklahoma. I stayed there while she went back to pack up our furniture and household belongings.

The woman that rented us the trailer agreed to leave an old sofa so that I would have something to sleep on until my furniture arrived. Imagine my surprise the first night when I found out that I was not the only one who used that sofa for a bed. I felt something crawl inside my nightshirt and I slapped it hard. Poor mouse never saw it coming.

I quickly learned that Oklahoma people have their unique form of entertainment. It is called "We Have Rotation." Almost nightly the television programming is interrupted by Doppler radar warnings. We have rotation would be the opening line. There was a new television newsperson that was almost as amused by these nightly warnings as I was. I heard him say one night, "we have rotation, we have liftoff, we have a problem."

I had not been there very long and one of the worst tornadoes that had ever struck Oklahoma came calling. It was over a mile wide and registered as an F5. It struck Moore, Oklahoma, and then traveled up the I44 corridor and hit Tulsa. Although the vast amount of the damage was in Moore, it was headed my way and people were calling and telling me to get out of that trailer.

I was probably 15 miles off of that path but I had no idea where I would have gone anyway. I didn't know anyone or where a public storm shelter might be located.

Once my wife and daughter arrived with her children they would stay up half the night listening to the weather radio and worrying about when the next tornado was going to touch down. I just went to bed. After all, I did not own a dog named Toto and I did not live in Kansas.

Chapter Twenty Five-Off To Oklahoma City

Towards the end of 1999, the company decided to open up the Oklahoma City Market. Garrett had applied for the Charlotte, North Carolina market and I naturally assumed that I would be given Tulsa. But it seems that another old nemesis, Alan Schmidt would throw a wrench into the cogs of that wheel. He had already decided to hire someone for the district manager position in Tulsa and wanted me to move to Oklahoma City but not as District Manager but rather as a field manager.

I was at the end of my rope at that point and I refused. If I was going to be a Field Manager, which was my present position, why should I have to move 90 miles to do it? I would just stay in Tulsa as a Field Manager.

Well, we argued back and forth and it looked like I would probably end up leaving the company and trying to find something else that paid somewhere close to what I was making.

Well, while this was going on Alan and the crew he had hired had managed to screw up the Oklahoma City market royally. He finally relented or more likely Barry Miller told him to relent and I was promoted to District Manager for Oklahoma City.

We had an odd method for collecting and keeping cash in those old markets. The day's receipts would be put into a manila envelope, sealed with the date and amount written on the outside. Then it would be locked in a cabinet under the front counter. Since the kiosk was in the middle of a store it seemed like it was a fairly secure system.

Every couple of weeks a manager would drive around to every kiosk and collect those envelopes and take them back to the office or in those first days to a motel room that Alan had rented for an office.

I had been involved in the picking up of envelopes in Tulsa and once or twice in Phoenix without ever having a dollar missing from those receipts. Imagine my surprise when I started picking up envelopes from kiosks in Oklahoma City only to discover that kiosk after kiosk had been broken into and the envelopes ripped open and the money was gone. I think the company lost something like $625 that day. So we figured that we could not wait another two weeks before collecting the envelopes and the next day we set out again to find the same thing had happened again.

So I called a locksmith and had him install more secure locks, this time with padlocks. This worked for a few days but then the crooks found that a bolt cutter could defeat padlocks.

Needless to say, most of my time was spent trying to catch the crooks instead of training a decent sales crew. We had a pretty good idea who the culprit was and when we started to zero in on him, he just stopped showing up to work. Security was notified to stop and detain him if he was seen entering the store and that put an end to the thefts for a while at least.

Once I did have time to start to work with the employees I quickly found that Alan had said, "oh Lord anybody" when he was hiring. I think his deciding factor must have been if they are breathing I will hire them.

About a month after I had assumed full control of the market we had a regional meeting in Tulsa. Alan came up to me and said, "You know we left you some pretty bad employees."

I said, "Yes and I fire one or two every day."

Barry Miller decided to do a secret shop on my market after about three months. We had not fully recovered from the terrible mess I found the market in but we were making headway. The one good thing he did find was that my people all tried to sell him accessories when he came to the booth even if they weren't particularly adept at selling phones.

We had our own office at that time and he came in and sat down across from my desk and told me that we could not continue to sell an average of one phone a day per kiosk I informed him that if I didn't have to spend half my time firing thieves and unproductive employees we could get production up.

The market did turn around soon after that and we became one of the best markets in the company. Part of that had to be because of the first field manager that I hired. His name was Brad Johnson and he came from working for one of the carriers in Tulsa.

When I interviewed him I asked him where he saw himself in five years and he told me he would be my boss. Someone once said to never fear hiring someone better than yourself and I hired Brad on the spot. I did, however, point out that the job he wanted would be the toughest job he ever had. Some of the questions I asked were: "Do you like to go out and have a nice quiet evening with someone without your phone ringing?"

Of course, the answer was yes. I said, "That will never happen again as long as you are a manager for Wireless Retail."

"Do you like to enjoy a meal without interruption?" Again the answer was yes.

"That will never happen as long as you are a manager with Wireless Retail."

Of course, he did not believe me. "Yeah, Yeah," He said.

Later he would tell me that for the first six months, he worked for me, there was never one day that he did not think about quitting.

My next hire as manager did not work out so well. He had worked for me in the Tulsa market and I was quite impressed with his maturity and work ethic when he applied I recommended we hire him. Alan objected strongly and in hindsight he was right. But I remember something that Barry Miller once told me about hiring people, "If you are right 50% of the time, you are ahead of the curve."

His name was Matt and he was a disaster. Although I had told him the same things that I had told Brad, he could not handle the pressure. One day he just did not show up for work. I would call his cell phone and it would go straight to voice mail. I would go out to look for him and could not find him. Finally, I came into the office and found his phone and keys on my desk. He never gave me an explanation. He just disappeared.

Looking back my choice of hires for management positions was about what Barry had said was above the curve 50%.

Oklahoma City was a huge market with 24 stores the farthest of them north in Ponca City almost to Kansas and the furthest south in Durant just north of the Texas border.

No field manager should have ever been required to supervise more than 10 stores but there were too many for two and too few for three so the market was broken up into 12 stores each for two field managers. Everything south of I40 was given to Brad Johnson and everything north of that divider was given to whoever happened to be the field manager at the time. I ran those 12 stores myself for the first six months after Matt disappeared.

Brad only worked for me for a little less than a year when he was called upon by Barry Miller to run the St. Louis marketplace. I did not want to lose him but I also was happy for him that he got his chance so quickly to become a district manager.

I needed another field manager and I did not have anyone in my market that I thought was qualified so I called the Tulsa District Agent, Kenda Cobb, and asked her if she might have someone that would be a good fit. She sent me a young man by the name of Patrick Blair. She told me that I might not like him because he was kind of shy but that he was a good salesperson and could train people.

She was right. My first indication was that Patrick would not cut it. He stammered a lot when answering my questions and I could see that he was so nervous that I was afraid he might pass out. But I could also see something in him that I could not quite put my finger on. I figured he couldn't be much worse than some of my other hires and so I gave him a chance.

Not one day did I ever regret that decision. We didn't always get along but he always did his very best to make me proud of him. I still count Patrick as one of my friends although I have not seen him in over five years.

I can't remember exactly when it happened but one day I got a call from Barry Miller asking me if I wanted to add to my market by taking over Wichita, Kansas. I certainly did not need any more stores but I thought that if I did a good enough job for the company they might someday promote me to regional director and so I said sure whatever they needed.

The market was actually under Brad Johnson's region and was managed (or not) by the District Manager out of Kansas City. There were 11 stores, 9 Wal-Marts, and 2 Sam's Clubs. I asked one of my better salespeople if he wanted to take on the Wichita market as a field manager and he accepted. So we put him up in an extended-stay motel until he could find a place and Tony Tovar (our regional director) the new manager and I all went up to try and straighten out the market.

Immediately it became certain that we had a huge problem that was not going to be solved without a complete overhaul of the sales staff. And so we called a meeting and Tovar got up and addressed the group and told them that the days of slacking off were over and that if anyone did not like it they could walk out the door right now. Half of the group got up and left.

So now we had 11 stores but only enough people to man half of them. So I called back to Oklahoma City and asked for volunteers to come up and help us until we could hire the right people. The most phones those 11 phones had sold in the market's history in any one day was 26 and for most of the days, it was less than one phone per store.

On our first day, we sold 33 phones out of that market.

The Kansas City District Manager believed that he could manage his markets by having the kiosks call a recorded message at the closing of the day. And he did not change the number to call when he lost Wichita. So of course, those that were leftover from his crew called in that first night to hear him ranting and raving.

"I don't know what they are doing in Wichita. I know they have Oklahoma City's best and brightest up there. But they have sold 33 phones their first day and God help you, people if they sell more than you do."

That was the only time in Wireless Retail history that not only was a market taken away from a district but moved to a different region as well.

Eventually, I also got the Tulsa Market making me a total of 83 stores that were under my direct supervision. That was more stores than a lot of regions had but I never was promoted to the regional director until just before the company went belly up.

Chapter Twenty Six-Over Expanded, Over Extended, and Gone

The thing that kills more small businesses than any other is expanding faster than your cash flow can keep up with. And that is exactly what killed Wireless Retail. Shortly after we opened the Tulsa market the local carrier absorbed the Phoenix market. At the time it did not seem too dire since we had just opened Tulsa, Oklahoma City was on the horizon and St. Louis had been opened before that. But all that was the start of the end though it did not seem so at the time.

The vast majority of those stores were Wal-Marts and I am sure that some hotshot accountant pointed out to Barry and Dan that they had far too many Walmart eggs in one basket. And they were probably right although you had to be careful that the baskets you added were not full of holes.

The Sam's Club addition was a great deal or, at least, it seemed to be from the standpoint of those of us looking in from the outside. Credit was far better at Sam's Club than at Wal-Marts and so activations per store were way up. For most of us, that was a welcome addition. But Sam's Club is still a part of Walmart although you don't want to ever tell that to Sam's general manager.

And what most of us did not realize was that there was a stipulation in Sam's contract that they could take over a certain amount of our kiosks each year and run them themselves.

Naturally, we didn't think that was a serious threat since we knew how to run a store within a store system better than anyone.

But I am sure that Dan and Barry were concerned about the possibility. And so they started branching out into areas that might have made sense to them but did not make any sense to those of us who worked with those kiosks daily.

One such experiment took place when they decided to try a kiosk in a Sears store in Oklahoma City. I could tell immediately that was not going to work as they placed our kiosk over in a corner behind the appliances where there was practically no foot traffic whatsoever. And in addition, they would not allow us to try and attract customers away from the kiosk nor would they allow us to use the PA system. I do not believe that we ever sold even one phone out of that store.

Another disaster that occurred was one that I never had any direct contact with. The company decided to try and sell phones out of Menard's Lumber Stores. Can you imagine customers going into a huge store like Menard's and after looking all over trying to find the things that they needed for their weekend handyman jobs listening to a spiel from someone trying to hawk a phone?

And about that time rumors were flying all over wondering if Wireless Retail was going to go belly up. Those rumors became more prevalent when Wal-Mart started taking over the kiosks in some of their stores and running them as Connection Centers.

Ah but not to worry we still had Sam's program. Or did we?

At some point in this march to going out of business, Wireless Retail had also started selling out of K-Marts and some other grocery stores. None of those enterprises were highly successful although Tim Denman swore the K-Marts in Denver, Colorado were producing over a hundred phones per month. At some point, I would have a shot at those Denver K-Marts and I can tell you that if they did produce over 100 phones per month per store it was fraud.

Another of their new store adventures was in a big box club called BJ's Wholesale Club. These were mostly in the northeast and when I heard they had got that contract I thought it was a good thing. I later learned that it was almost as much a disaster as Menards.

In fact, the first time I ever saw a BJ s was in Mayfield, Ohio. When I pulled into the parking lot I counted three cars and figured I might have trouble selling phones out of that store.

Then the rumors started flying that Wireless Retail had borrowed 50 million dollars from one of the carriers and guaranteed they would sell huge quantities of their phones to repay the money. I guess I should have known what was happening when we started getting instructions to sell one carrier over the other three.

The story goes that the carrier called in the loan when we did not hit the quota that had been set for them. The next rumor came along that we were in the process of selling off the Sam's Club program to Radio Shack to get the money to repay said loan. At that point, some of the rats began leaving the ship and if I had been smart I might have gone with them. But I was sure that if Radio Shack did buy the Sam's program they would need sales managers so I should still have a job.

Then the actual word did come down that there were going to be two separate conference calls, one for the managers that would be going over to Radio Shack and one for the managers that would be staying with Wireless Retail. To my chagrin I was on the second call, the one staying with Wireless Retail.

I could not believe it since with the amount of Wal-Marts we had lost and the loss of Sam's clubs there was no market left for me to run. From a monstrous market that once had 83 stores under my supervision, there was not much of anything left.

What it looked like to me was that I would be doing mop-up duty, closing kiosks, salvaging equipment, and sending back whatever was left over to Phoenix.

Eventually, what they did was give me all of the K-Marts and the few Wal-Marts that were not productive enough for Wal-Mart to run by themselves. That was when I got a chance to look at those fantastic

K-Marts in Denver, Colorado. None of them had been manned for months and in some cases, the kiosks had been put out back by the dumpsters. Of course, the first order of business was to try and soothe the anger of the store managers who had seen no Wireless Retail employees in their stores in months. It amazed me that if those stores had been selling such a huge amount of phones as Denman had claimed why were they not manned?

Most of my managers had been assigned to Radio Shack but there were a few that stayed with Wireless Retail including a young woman who had been a field manager in Wichita, Kansas. She was as close as anyone that worked for me and so I asked her if she would take over those K-Marts in Denver.

None of the markets were producing and so since the company had no more carrots they decided to wield the stick. Any kiosk that did not sell a phone in a day had to be on a conference call the following morning at 7 AM. Everyone hated those calls because they were beat-em-up calls. In other words, what in the hell is wrong with you that you couldn't even sell one phone yesterday? That got old fast and people started quitting left and right. That included my field manager from Wichita. I finally got one of my old managers from Oklahoma City to go up there and she did a fair job with an impossible task. But eventually, even those stores were closed up.

There was nothing left to manage in Oklahoma, Kansas, or Colorado and so the company offered to move me to Cleveland, Ohio to manage 13 K-Marts and 5 BJ Wholesale Clubs. I didn't have a choice at that point so once again we packed up the truck for another move.

I found a house to rent in Parma, Ohio, and signed a two-year lease with the caveat that I could break the lease if I had to move for employment reasons. This was in April of 2005. And then the company folded completely on July 1 of 2005.

The first we heard about it was one night late in June they had a conference call with all the managers. It went something like this:

"Wait until the close of business today and then call all your K-Mart people and tell them not to come to work tomorrow. But don't worry we still have the BJ Clubs so you managers will be okay.

Then on the first of July, we had another conference call. "At the close of business, today call your remaining employees and tell them not to come to work tomorrow. You, managers, are required to stay on until you can clean out those kiosks, salvage what you can, and ship it back to corporate.

At that point, I was in a real pickle. I was in a strange city, with no job and a two-year lease on a house that soon I would not be able to afford. My one saving grace was that they did give me a severance package of one month's base salary for every year I had been with the company. That was ten months' base pay, which kept me going for a while.

Chapter Twenty-Seven-Brad's Prophesy Comes True

Of course, I started calling everyone that I knew in the wireless industry from those on the Radio Shack side to former carriers. There were no takers.

So my wife and I decided to take a trip to Phoenix to visit one of our children. We were gone for a week and while I was there I stopped in at the Radio Shack regional office to see if there might be a position open somewhere within the company. But then I got the surprise of my life. They did not rehire former employees and since I had worked for the company for a short while in the mid-1990s I was disqualified.

I got a call from Brad Johnson and he told me that he was no longer with Radio Shack and was in the process of transferring to a new company. He suggested that I call the field manager in Cleveland to see if he might have a kiosk manager position open. It was a long way down from regional director, my last title with Wireless Retail but I needed a job.

I finally reached him but was told all he had available was a sales rep position and I told him I was not interested.

When we boarded the plane back to Cleveland, I, of course, turned off my wireless phone. When we pulled up to the gate in Cleveland I switched my phone back on and had three voice messages. They were all from Brad Johnson who had prophesied that he would be my boss someday.

The first one said, "Wayne, call me." The second said Wayne call me now." and the third said, "Damn it call me."

For some reason I got the impression he wanted to talk with me so, I called him back. I was surprised to learn that he was now working for a company called Wireless Advocates and was a regional manager for the Midwest.

It seemed that the field manager for Cleveland had discovered how much work it took to roll out a market and had quit without notice so now Brad needed someone to oversee a seven-store market in Ohio and Indiana, which was just rolling out. All of the kiosks were inside Costco.

This company did not allow even regional managers to hire their own District Managers so Brad sent a recruiter in to interview me. When he was finished he handed me a packet of paperwork to fill out and a drug test form to be taken to the local laboratory immediately so I figured I had the job.

The job was similar to what I had done in the past with the exception that we were not allowed to pass out flyers, make announcements, or sell more than six feet away from the booth location. So our success or failure was dependent upon where the Costco God deemed it to place our kiosks. The managers that cared about our success allowed us a spot on one of the end caps. Those that did not care or some that would rather we were not in their stores at all would hide the kiosk behind some huge display as far from the main aisle as they could find.

One thing that became immediately evident was that credit approval was not a problem when you sold phones inside Costco. When we were in Wal-Mart credit approval usually came back 1 approval for every 5 applications although there were some stores where it was closer to 1 in 10. In Sam's Club the credit approval was one out of two but in Costco, if you had a credit decline once a week you were shocked.

The first two stores that rolled out were in Cleveland and then two more in Cincinnati and then two more in Indianapolis and then one in Merrillville, Indiana, which was almost to Chicago.

Most of the employees had already been interviewed and hired by my predecessor and unlike Alan Schmidt, he had done a fairly good job.

I quickly learned that this position did not pay nearly as well as even the field manager's job I had with Wireless Retail. I think the lowest amount of money I ever made with them was $75000 and with Wireless Advocates, I was lucky to make $55000 even with bonuses.

Eventually, the market expanded to 11 stores when three were added in Pittsburgh, Pa. and one in Columbus, and one in Louisville, Kentucky. I lost the Merrillville store when I took the three Pennsylvania stores.

I ran that market for just over two years, which worked out well for my lease on the house we were living in. At some point, however, Brad called me and asked if I thought I would like to take over the Phoenix market. I knew that my wife wanted to go back to the southwest and so I agreed to go down and talk with the southwest regional manager. I knew within the first five minutes that we would never get along working together and so after talking with Janice, I turned down the position.

Brad called me and asked me why I did not want to take the job and I told him that I just could not imagine being able to work for the regional manager there. He told me that the company wanted me to take that market and that perhaps there was another option. He said that he had asked to have that market added to his region.

Eventually, that came to pass and I agreed to move to Phoenix and take over the north side of the market. But I wasn't allowed to move immediately. The company expected that I would find my replacement for the Ohio, Indiana, Pennsylvania, and Kentucky markets. And that wasn't the easiest task that I had ever undertaken. I remember what

Ross Perot had said when they asked him to run for President of the United States. "If a person is qualified for the job they would not want it."

I had almost given up on finding someone that would be good at doing the job and someone crazy enough to want it. But eventually, I did find a Sprint manager that applied and somehow went all the way through the process and the company offered her the job.

But now it became my job to train her which would not have been too difficult but the company wanted her to work in a kiosk for two weeks before she even started training as a district manager.

Suffice it to say that eventually, I did end up in the Phoenix marketplace. I spent a few days just traveling around from kiosk to kiosk and it did not take me long to understand that I had taken over a market much like Oklahoma City had been years prior. I would go to secret shop a kiosk and find it empty. I would wait for an hour or so and still, no one would show up.

Well, there is a pretty apropos saying. "You can't sell phones from a kiosk if you are not there."

Before I had even taken over the market officially I called a meeting of all the employees. It had to be a split session since someone had to man the kiosk at all times. I came in with great enthusiasm because I could see the potential in that market. There was a huge amount of foot traffic and if our people approached everyone that came by they were bound to sell phones.

The company had a firm rule for each person that worked for them and that was that they were required to "Perimeter Sell." That meant that unless they were with a customer they needed to be outside of the kiosk interacting with the people passing their locations. And I managed to convince those salespeople that even though their previous managers had never required them to do it, it was a rule and I expected that they would abide by it. I also showed them how to increase their sales by writing down any offer they might make to a customer and showing them the offer in writing.

For the year before me taking over the market, the 9 stores had never sold more than 1400 phones in a month. So of course, both the employees and I were shocked when they got their monthly quota and it was 1700 phones. That meant that almost every kiosk would have to sell 200 phones. Of course, some of them were better than others so the goals were not evenly distributed. A couple of the stores ended up with a quota of 280 phones and some of them with a quota of 150. Of course, the stores with the higher quota went ballistic but again I managed to calm them down, and lo and behold the market did reach that lofty quota and surpassed it.

Everyone was happy until they saw the next month's quota. The company had raised it to 2100 phones for the market. That was completely stupid and although I did not use that word I told the home office that it was unreasonable. I further told them that if they wanted these people to produce that they needed to ease them up to what they wanted not hit them over the head with it.

The home office refused and said the goal is the goal and you have to reach it if you wanted to keep your job. We didn't come close and never came close to the 1700 phones again. No one could have hit the quotas that Wireless Advocates sent down unless they fired every person in that market and started over with an entirely new crew.

As the saying goes "attitude is everything" and the attitude in that market was that the company did not give a damn about its people. No matter how positive I was, they were positive that I was full of shit.

I did as good a job as possible and I managed to stay on for a couple of years. One of the top people from corporate would come into my market every few months. They would go around and observe what my people were doing and never would find anything seriously wrong. They were out perimeter selling and making good sales pitches but they just were not getting the results. Of course, the executive would always ask me what I thought the problem was and the first time I told them it all came back to that second month's quota. Of course, they didn't want to hear that so I quit telling them.

I knew that I was going to get fired. I had given everything I had but it just was not enough. And of course, that was around the time when the entire country was headed for a huge recession. None of that mattered to Wireless Advocates. Produce or get out was their unwritten motto.

I don't know when I discovered that I hated my job but I do know that it was long before I took over that Phoenix market. I remember a time being in a motel room in Indianapolis and wishing that I had a bottle of sleeping pills so I could take them all and not have to wake up to go to work in the morning.

This was by far the worst job I ever had with the possible exception of dumping tomatoes off of a truck for 16 hours a day at the South Dayton Canning Factory. Imagine a sales management position that was so terrible that it rivaled that.

What I do know is that by the time they finally fired me, I was so depressed that not a day passed without me considering eating my gun.

All companies have turnover but usually not in the upper management positions but Wireless Advocates was so hard to work for that they couldn't even keep regional managers, no less District Managers.

Chapter Twenty Eight-Back to Selling Insurance or Not

I was nearing retirement age but not quite and so I needed something to do. I thought about going back into the life insurance business and I put in my application to several different companies. Of course, I had to get my license back and so I decided to take a course that prepared people for taking the life and health license in Arizona.

It is far more difficult to get a license to sell insurance now than it was back in 1966 but I still managed to pass the test on my first try.

The first company that offered me a position I found was more of a telemarketing outfit and I knew that wouldn't work. I hate receiving sales calls and so I figured I wouldn't be much good at making them.

I finally accepted a position with Pennsylvania Life Insurance Company although I never did sell a life insurance policy for them. What I did sell were policies written under the Medicare Advantage part of the Medicare law.

My problem was that the company I worked for did not believe in giving leads in the Phoenix marketplace. They would work for a week in Northern Arizona and then a week in Southwestern Arizona and then a week in Yuma, Arizona.

I suppose that would not have been too bad if they had paid anything for selling their product. Originally they had told me that they paid $180 for each policy sold but when I started getting my commission checks they were for $40.

"Oh, we had to change our commission schedule," They said.

I was paying more for gas than I was making in commission so that ended my sales career.

Chapter Twenty-Nine-Poems, Songs, and Novels

I had always wanted to try and write a book but until the computer came along I never got very far. My first computer was one that an electronics house sold me. It had a 20-megabyte hard drive and word perfect miraculously came with it. The salesman told me that 20 megabytes were more memory than I could ever possibly use. Of course, today, the software for word perfect would take up far more than that before you wrote anything.

I had always thought that some of the things that went on in the world were strange, to say the least, and so I started writing a book entitled "Common Sense Solutions for Complex Problems." Some of the topics were the national debt and strange laws that were enacted in the state of Arizona. I even had a section entitled "Sex". That section simply said, "I don't know anything about sex, but I was told you had to include it for your book to sell." Many years later that statement was proved true.

I wish that I had printed out a copy of that book but alas my hard drive fried and the book was lost. I never did get back to serious writing for quite a few years. And then one day I decided to write an article and send it to Outdoor Life magazine to see if they would print it. It was entitled the perfect hunt and was a parody of many of the articles that I saw in those sporting magazines. According to most of the articles, everything always went exactly as planned. In my hunting experiences, that was completely the opposite. Murphy's Law almost always applied.

"If something can go wrong, it will, and usually at the worst possible moment."

It was rejected and they even sent my paper copy back to me. I sent a joke or two to Reader's Digest as well and they were also rejected although they did not tell me why.

Here is the story I sent to Outdoor Life as I remember it. I am sure I left out a lot, however.

The Perfect Hunt?

I grew up reading outdoor magazines and was always amazed that everything went off exactly as was planned. In my life, that has never been the case. So the title above is written with tongue in cheek.

I saw him coming through the trees. He was the biggest buck I had ever seen in my life. I carefully raised my gun and pulled the trigger. And then the roar of the alarm clock shocked me out of the dream. Another perfect hunt ruined.

It was the opening day of deer season in Allegheny County, New York. I guess the year was probably 1967 or 1968. I had a job as a life insurance salesman and had talked my General Manager, Bill Pauling, and my District Manager, Lloyd Lyke into taking the day off and going hunting for deer with me.

I had purchased an old house on six acres of land in a dot on the map called Obi, New York. Across from the house was a large meadow, where I had been watching two small herds of deer all summer. Behind the meadow was a small creek that ran along the base of a high hill. Every evening the deer would appear from the far left corner of the meadow and proceed to eat their fill of the lush green grass. I figured that I knew exactly where they got water and where they bedded down in the morning. And so I plotted out the "perfect hunt".

Problem number one occurred when I crawled out of bed at 4 am to prepare breakfast for my fellow hunters and myself. When I had gone to sleep the night before we had about six inches of snow on the ground and I had high hopes that we would be able to track a deer should we hit it but not kill it immediately. But during the night, the weather had warmed and a warm rain had moved in. As I looked out my side door I could see that almost all of the snow was gone and a heavy fog hung in the air. I had a bad feeling at that time but I could not quite put my finger on why.

Lloyd and Bill showed up and as we ate a huge meal consisting of pancakes, eggs, and bacon we talked through the game plan for the day. One of us would go down the road a couple of miles where there was an old bridge that he could use to cross the creek. Two others would go directly from my house and cross the creek on foot. Normally that would not have been a big problem as the creek was relatively shallow most of the time.

Lloyd had volunteered to be the "dog". That is the one to drive the deer towards Bill and me. Lloyd was to go down the road about two miles where there was an old bridge on which he could cross the creek. He was to wait there about a half-hour, which I figured would give Bill and me enough time to cross the creek, climb halfway up the hill and get into position. The deer should come right by our location for an easy shot. Normally this might have worked.

I had checked the creek a couple of days before opening day and it was low enough to cross in several places by simply putting garbage bags over our boots and walking across. But when Bill and I reached the creek I could see that we had a severe problem with our plan. The creek was now a roaring turbulent mass of water. We took off our boots, put our socks inside them, and tossed them across to the other side. Then we rolled up our pants as far as possible and began to cross the creek holding our shotguns above our heads and hoping that we did not hit a pool that was so deep that our coats would get wet as well. By the time, we had reached the other side we were wet, cold, and had lost a ton of time that should have been used to get into position.

We were still putting on our boots when I heard the fake barking of a dog and I realized that Lloyd was taking his role of the dog seriously.

I also realized that unless we took off at almost a dead run we would never reach the spot where I had doped out that the deer would cross.

Now problem number two comes into play. Bill had spent most of his life selling insurance and very little of it climbing hills. We had barely reached a quarter of the way up the hill when Bill announced, "This looks like a good place, and I will wait here."

And so alone, I proceeded as quickly as possible to try to reach the spot I had staked out earlier. I had almost made it when through the brush; I saw the waving white tails as the deer raced away through the woods.

Now the perfect plan was completely gone. With nothing better in mind, I found a good vantage point and settled down to wait. My only hope was that maybe someone else might move those deer back toward my location.

Now I have to tell you that waiting was never my strong suit. I remember when I was a kid, my neighbor told my father that he could always depend on me to get bored and start moving through the woods and usually drive a deer right to him.

So, by nine in the morning, I was ready to find the other guys, get a cup of coffee and form another plan. So as quietly as I could I made my way back toward where I had left Bill.

When I arrived at the spot where I had left Bill, he was not there. Thinking he must be close I let out a whistle and waited for a reply. None came so I let out another whistle but instead of hearing another whistle, I heard four quick blasts from a 12-gauge shotgun. After waiting another ten minutes, I made my way toward where the gun had gone off. I had only gone a few yards when I came upon Bill.

"Was that you that shot?" I asked.

"Yes," he replied. "I shot at a buck. He was about a six-point and he was all white around his nose."

"Really?" I asked. "How close were you to this deer?"

"Pretty close", was his reply.

After determining which way the deer went, I decided to try and follow him for a way, just in case Bill had hit him. The trail was fairly easy to follow in the wet leaves and several times he had crossed where there was still enough snow so that I could determine that the deer had survived his encounter with Bill unscathed. Below me was an old logging trail that I figured I could follow back around the hill. I was about 30 yards away and decided to stop and survey my surroundings. As I rested against a large tree I heard several shots. Although they were a long way off I had been trained that when you hear gunfire you should stay where you are and be alert.

About 20 minutes had passed, and I was just getting ready to move when off to my left I spotted movement on the logging trail. The first real sign that I had it was a deer was when I saw the sunlight gleaming off of his antlers. I raised my gun, took the safety off, and waited. It was not long before the deer came straight past my location. I took careful aim and fired. He went down with the impact but almost immediately regained his footing and started down the hill away from me. Although I was sure I had dealt a lethal blow, he was going the wrong way and I knew I would have to drag him back up that hill to get him home. So I emptied my Winchester at him. He finally fell and lay still. I refilled my shotgun and carefully made my way to where he lay.

As I reached the deer, I was surprised to note that he was a five-point buck, all white around the edge of his nose. Undoubtedly he was the same deer Bill had shot at earlier. And incidentally, he was only hit once. None of the subsequent five shots had touched him.

It took me a few minutes to field dress the deer and then I decided to try and call Bill to help drag the deer up the hill. I yelled, "Bill" but there was no answer. I waited a few minutes and tried again "BILL" but still no answer. So I grabbed the carcass by the antlers and started the long tedious task of dragging the deer up that steep hill. I imagine it took me over an hour with frequent stops to try and summon Bill but I got no reply until I finally topped the hill and then by magic Bill appeared. As he got to my location he looked at the deer and exclaimed, "That is him, that is the deer I shot at."

My deer hunting was over for the year as there was a one-deer limit and so Bill and I decided to take the deer home, get something to eat and then try and find Lloyd. It was all downhill so it did not take long to drag the deer to the edge of the creek. Now the fun began. I gave Bill my shotgun, took off my boots, rolled up my pants, took my belt and attached it to the deer's horns, and proceeded to step off into the water. I had just managed to get the deer into the stream when the belt broke and the deer started to float downstream. Giving caution to the wind, I plowed after him and went in up to my neck. Not having to worry about getting wet I raced after the floating deer and managed to get him to the other bank. Lloyd told me afterward that he wished he could have witnessed this event as he would have fired a few shots into the water in front of the deer and yelled, "look at that buck swimming the river". As for me, I only wish I had taken a rope so I could have crossed the stream before pulling the deer in behind me.

Then I ran into a period where I decided that I wanted to be more romantic in my life and so I began writing poems to my wife for special occasions, anniversaries, Valentine's day, and sometimes just to say I love you. None of those poems are around today and my poetic mind, I believe died with the vast amount of pain pills I took while waiting for back surgery.

One thing that did survive, however, was the four songs that I wrote. I remember coming home one night and my grandchild, Christopher was climbing on the back of our sofa. My wife remarked, "Christopher you may be a little angel but you don't have your wings yet."

I thought that would be a great title for a song and so I set down and wrote the song, "God Should Give Small Angels Little Wings." I joined the Arizona Song Writers Association thinking that I might be able to sell that one but without success. Anyway here it is:

First Verse
We have a little angel that believes that he can fly
He flaps his arms and turns his head to look up in the sky
As if to ask from heaven just a gentle breeze to bring
God should give small angles little wings
Chorus
Wings to help their balance and wings to bring them joy
Wings to help protect a little girl or little boy
But wings were not provided to keep them safe from harm
So God gave them what's second best, a loving parent's arms
Second Verse
He's always building ladders out of chairs and blocks and toys.
He sometimes scares us half to death but he brings us so much joy
His curls must hide his halo as he does these risky things.
God should give small angels, little wings.
Repeat Chorus
Third Verse
The radio is playing some music soft and low
We hear the dishes rattle and we know we have to go
He's standing on the table and he's dancing as they sing
God should give small angels little wings
Repeat Chorus
Fourth Verse
There's a railing on his crib and there're gates across the doors
There're pillows lying everywhere he's almost fell before
They probably won't protect him cause he climbs on everything
God should give small angels little wings
Repeat Chorus
I guess I felt bad for writing a song for one member of the family
and so I figured that I should write one that included everyone, so I sat
down and wrote, "I'm Just a Grandpa Now". Here it is:
First Verse

I've spent my life a dreaming of fortune and of fame
I thought it was important, to have a famous name
So people who'd looked down on me could come to understand.
That crazy fool they saw in school now had the upper hand
Chorus
Those dreams did not come true, nobody knows my name
Except a precious few, I have no money and no fame
I'm just a grandpa now, one that has come to see
There's nothing in this world I'd rather be.
Second Verse
I wish instead of dreaming, I'd spent more years of life
Realizing happiness with my children and my wife
Money can't buy happiness, it won't your life enrich
But the way you live and the love you give
Are the things that make you rich
Second Chorus
My dreams have all come true, ten smiling faces to adore (when this was originally written it was 3 smiling faces)
They are the precious few that play upon my floor
I'm just a grandpa now, one that has come to see
There's nothing in this world I'd rather be
Third Verse
When you spend your life a dreaming it's hard to comprehend
That the things that are important are your family and your friends
They never will look down on you, their shoulders are not cold
They're always there and they always care even when you're old
Third Chorus
My dreams have all come true, I'm rich but not with wealth
I have a precious few, that love me for myself
I'm just a grandpa now, one that has come to see
There's nothing in this world I'd rather be.

I continued to try and write songs for a while and I wrote one about a cowboy one day. It was during the OJ Simpson trial and everyone was captivated by it. I asked my daughter if she wanted to hear it and she said if it is not about OJ no.

I was getting ready to go out and deliver some cable boxes and so I took a pen and pad with me. At every red light, I would jot down a little bit of what would become "No Way OJ Could Have Done It". Here is that song"

First Verse

They found them on June 13th, two bodies lying still upon the ground

And they said the barking of a dog led them to the grisly scene they found

They sent out four detectives to go and notify the next of kin

But they jumped the wall and found the glove and knew from that time on that it was him

Chorus

But no way OJ could have done it

He simply had no time to do the crime

No way OJ could have done it

But you'll never get a cop to change his mind

Second Verse

A jury was impaneled; Judge Ito sat so proud behind the bench

Marsha and Chris Darden told the world that they had the evidence

But their mountain slowly crumbled into a very tiny pile of stone

And all that time, a year or more, poor OJ sat in his cell alone

Second Chorus

But no way OJ could have done it

He simply had no time to do the crime

No way OJ could have done it

But Marsha Clark will never change her mind

Third Verse
We'll never know who did it because the county wasted so much precious time
They never looked for someone else for he was always guilty in their minds
The only thing that saved him was his money and his fame or so they say
But the jury said not guilty and the Juice was on the loose that very day
Third Chorus
But no way OJ could have done it
He simply had no time to do the crime
No way OJ could have done it
But some people still refuse to change their mind
The following song I just wrote for fun. I had no special reason for writing it. It is called "Girls Don't Wear Heels". Here it is.
First Verse
It used to make me happy, to stand out by the street
Watching all the girls go by, it used to be a treat
To see them in their mini-skirts and heels three inches high
But the world has changed so much it seems it makes me want to cry
First Chorus
Girls don't wear heels. They wear the boxes on their feet
They say it feels, so comfy and so neat
I'll just stay home and I'll watch the Oprah show
If you want to see high-heels a transvestite you must know
Second Verse
I had a dream the other night while lying in my bed
Visions of the future kept running through my head
I saw a great big wedding on the upper side of town
But the bride was wearing tennis shoes beneath her wedding gown

Second Chorus
Girls don't wear heels, they wear the boxes on their feet
They say it feels so comfy and so neat
I'll just stay home and I'll watch the Sally show
If you want to see high heels a transvestite you must know
Third Verse
It used to make me happy to see the girls downtown
They took some pride in what they wore, no sweatsuits could be found
Today I just don't go downtown, I don't believe I can
If you see a woman all dressed up it's probably a man
Third Chorus
Girls don't wear heels, they wear the boxes on their feet
They say it feels, so comfy and so neat
I'll just stay home and watch the Sally show
If you want to see high heels a transvestite you must know
The Great American Novel

I guess I have written a few other songs over the years but nothing worth including within the pages of this book. My second attempt at writing the great American Novel took place while I was district manager in Oklahoma City working for Wireless Retail. I did not have a computer at home and so I would stay after work and write a few pages of what I thought at the time would be an erotic story. I did not dream that it would end up being over 77000 words long. It did not have a title at that point but one night Patrick Blair came in and asked me what I was still doing there. I explained that I was trying to write a story and he said what kind of story.

I told him I was not 100% sure at that point and he asked if he could read what I had written. So I printed it out and gave it to him. Unbeknownst to me, he shared it with one of the women that worked in the office complex. She, in turn, shared it with two other women that worked there. I didn't find out until a few days later that not only was Patrick reading the story but so were three other women. So now I figured that I had to change it so that it might not be quite so raw.

Every day Patrick and these women would meet me outside. As Patrick and I smoked our cigarettes the girls would tell me about what they had read so far and commend me, or critique me on where they thought the story should go. Of course, I changed the story so that it did not go in any of the directions they suggested just so they would be surprised when the next segment came out.

It took me three months to complete that book and when I was through I was quite sure that it would be a best seller. It had everything that a good novel should have, a little sex, a little violence, and a lot of twists and turns.

So I started looking for a publisher that would, at least, look at it. All I received were rejection letters except for one that said they would publish one hundred copies if I would pay them $2700. So I gave up on the idea of being a best-selling novelist. But this time, I, at least, made sure that the story was backed up on a secondary hard drive so that it would not be lost like the previous book I had written.

I had an idea for a second book but after the amount of work I had put into this one, it got shelved for a lot of years. It was not until 2008 when I discovered self-publishing through Amazon.com that I even tried to get the book published.

With my daughter's help, I managed to figure out how to set up an account and upload my book file. I didn't have any idea of how to create a cover and not much of an idea of how to format the book so that it was readable. It is no surprise that it has never sold very many copies. Plus I still haven't figured out how to use keywords to attract a large audience.

I gave up writing for a long time after that. Oh, I wrote a few stories just for my amusement but nothing that I wanted to submit to anyone for publication.

Then one spring my daughter told me in casual conversation that a friend of hers was making some money writing what she called smut. I didn't think too much of it at the time but then I thought, I could write smut. And I did. I presently have 40 books published under, fiction, and erotica on several platforms.

Of course, I write under a pen name, which I am not going to divulge here. If you knew me back in the early years of the Internet you might be able to figure it out.

Chapter Thirty My Views on Religion

For the first twelve years of my life, I was required by my mother to attend religious services on Sunday, Tuesday evenings, and Thursday evenings. And most Saturdays were spent going door to door preaching the "Good News of God's Kingdom".

I never questioned whether what I was being taught was true or not, the only thing that I was positive of was I would have rather spent that time hunting, fishing, playing baseball, or reading about one of the three.

My mother was devout but I don't think my father was quite so enamored with religion. I never heard him say that he did not want to go to services or out in the ministry for that matter but I got the impression that if he could use the farm schedule to avoid it he would.

Finally, when I was twelve years old I decided that I did not want to continue going. My mother, of course, was adamant that I continue but my father stepped in and overruled her.

I have to admit looking back however that I got more out of the experience than I might have expected. For one thing, I learned to read much earlier than I would have otherwise. By the time I went to Kindergarten, I already knew how to read fluently, a product of having read the Bible from the time I could comprehend words.

One other thing I learned was that people do not like having someone come to their door to talk with them about religion. I sometimes wonder if that was not why I had very few friends when I was growing up.

A lot of those negative feelings come from people who do not understand the Jehovah's Witness religion. I have heard things like, "They are not Christians." Nothing could be further from the truth. They believe that their salvation can only come from recognizing Jesus Christ's sacrifice as the only way into God's Kingdom. They do however not believe that Christ is God taking what is said in John 10:36 instead.

"Say ye of him, whom the Father hath sanctified, and sent into the world, Thou blasphemest; because I said, I am the Son of God?" And as such, they do not believe in the Trinity as most mainline religions do.

I am not sure it matters. What I am sure of is that most Jehovah's Witnesses are as devout in their belief in God and his son Jesus Christ as any other religion.

Does doctrine matter, perhaps, perhaps not? One doctrine that I could never wrap my mind around is one that almost every religion teaches and that is that the wicked go to a place of eternal torment. But all these religions also teach that "God is Love". One seems to contradict the other. How could a loving God sentence his or her children to a place where they would never be allowed to die but have to keep suffering immense torture for the remainder of time?

I do remember one day when I was out preaching to anyone that would listen I asked that question of an old man. "Do you really believe a loving God would send his children to a place of eternal torment?" His answer was, "I hope so because there are a lot of people I would like to have go there." I suspect at that moment I was one of those people.

I am not going to argue the merits or lack thereof of any specific religion. What I will argue is that I believe that at least at some point there existed a higher power. I say this because I cannot imagine how this universe could have come into existence in such perfection without it being planned by someone or something with an extremely high level of intelligence.

I hear people say that the universe came about by a giant explosion, which scattered the parts throughout the different solar systems. But I have never seen an accident that produced perfection.

I just cannot accept that one solar system could have been produced with the sun and the various planets and their moons all ending up in the exact spot they needed to be to keep rotating around each other no less the countless solar systems that exist somewhere in outer space.

So I do not doubt in my mind that God existed. What I am not so sure of is whether that same God influences our present lives. I used to think that if someone truly believed in God that they were better people than those that did not. However, looking at how some Muslims slaughter innocent women and children in the name of their religion I can no longer say that. In addition, some so-called Christian religions do terrible things in the name of their God.

As I look around me and see the suffering of so many children in the world I wonder why God does not intervene on their behalf. Perhaps he or she is waiting for a specified time before he or she finally steps in and sets things right. Again I don't have that answer.

Chapter Thirty-One Politics and Conspiracy Theories

Upfront let me say that I believe that both political parties are corrupt and need to be disbanded. Both of them try to convince us that they care about "the middle class" but nothing could be further from the truth. All they care about is staying in office so that they can continue living off of the public dole. I am not sure when the last semi-honest man was elected President but I think it was a long time before I was born. In fact, I doubt that anyone is alive today that has seen a truly good President. One note, this book was written before Donald Trump was elected President in 2016.

I wrote a satire not long ago and posted it on Facebook. Here it is for your amusement:

A little history of a once-great nation

Once upon a time, there was a great country founded on the principle that if you worked hard you would have the opportunity to succeed. There was no guarantee that you would succeed only that you would have such an opportunity. It worked exceedingly well for some time. Some men and women built businesses in the large towns and cities and others went into the wilderness to forge out land that they could call their own. Some of them got rich and others did not fair as well but no one blamed the rich people for the misfortunes of the poor.

At some point, the rich people in the north of the country got angry with the rich people in the south of the country and before long half, a million Americans died of their wounds. A tall homely man in a black hat came along to lead the rich people of the north. In the process, he appointed a drunk to be the head of the Northern army, and before the booze ran out the Southern people were whipped. Now should have come the time for healing but an actor decided to kill the tall homely man with the black hat and his successor proved to be corrupt and the rich people in the north were able to make sure that only those people who were on the side of the north could become rich. So many of the lazy people who lived in the north put their few belongings in carpet bags and headed south where they were given the money and property of those who used to own it.

The successor to the man in the black hat was not re-elected but in his stead, the drunk who led the army of the north was put in his place. He was just as corrupt as his predecessor and so no healing took place during his presidency. And the lazy northern poor were still given what the rich southern people had worked hard for. About, this time, many people discovered that hard work was not the secret to success but rather knowing someone in power was the secret to success. Why work if someone would give you something just because you supported them?

For some time after that, no great leader stepped forward or if they did they were not elected. I believe this because I don't know anyone who has any idea what the next 6 or 7 presidents did while they were in office. Then along came someone who is best known for his charge up San Juan Hill. He decided that corporations were evil and that if you had a lot of money it should be taken away from you and given to those that did not have so much money. You no longer had to be a rich Southerner for the government to divest you of your money; you just needed to be rich.

I am not sure what the next president did although he is best known for being so fat that someone had to pry him out of the White House bathtub.

Then along came what we would today call the first real socialist president. This great American found even better ways to steal from those who had as well as those who did not. He enacted the Income Tax so that everyone that had any money of any kind would have to give it to the government. And he also created the Federal Reserve so that he could manipulate how much the money he stole from the people would be worth.

The nice thing was that you did not have to be Republican or Democrat to be evil; you just had to be president. The corrupt man that took the place of the tall homely man with the black hat was a Democrat, the drunk that took his place was a Republican as was the one who charged up San Juan Hill, and then the income tax creator was a Democrat. So until this point in history, both parties were good at taking money from some people and giving it to other people. Of course, most of the money, they took from others went into their own pockets or the pockets of their friends and family.

And another funny thing happened back there. The members of the House and Senate used to work together, usually for their own good and to the detriment of the people but work together nonetheless.

So this gets you up to date on the first hundred years or so of the history of the once-upon-a-time nation. Frankly, I am too worn out to finish the story. Perhaps some of you other storytellers could take over for me.

Chapter Thirty Two-My Political Leanings Today

I guess I lean a lot more toward the Republicans than I do the Democrats. In actuality, I would much prefer that The Libertarian Party would become strong enough to contend in national elections. But I am realistic enough to know that it does not matter who gets elected. I heard a joke one time many years ago of a pollster that went out in the countryside to get people's views on an upcoming election.

It seems an up-and-coming young man was running against a career politician that everyone knew was a crook. The pollster asked an old farmer who he was going to vote for and the farmer told him he would vote for the career politician. The pollster pressed the issue to try and find out the farmer's reasoning and this is what the farmer told him.

"If they ain't spoiled when they go in they are spoiled when they come out and there is no reason to spoil a good man."

I honestly cannot say that I remember a politician in any major office in this country that did not get elected by lying about themselves or their opponent. But the crops that we have now are the worst by far that I have ever seen.

What I cannot understand is why everyone that calls themselves a Democrat always agrees and everyone that calls themselves a Republican always agrees. For instance, when the "Affordable Care Act" was passed not one Republican voted for it. How is that possible? Surely there must have been one Republican that thought that it was a good bill. And on the other side of the aisle, certainly, there must have been a few Democrats who thought it was a lousy idea.

Of course, the truth is they had no idea whether it was a good bill or a bad bill because nobody had time to read it. In the immortal words of Nancy Pelosi, "We have to pass the bill to find out what is in it."

Here is my opinion of that law. First, it is misnamed. It did absolutely nothing to make health care more affordable. Doctors did not lower their fees and hospitals did not lower their rates. So maybe it should have been called: The law to subsidize some people's insurance while vastly overcharging others. Secondly, anytime the government gets involved in anything it is bound to be bad. What is the biggest lie ever told? "I am from the government and I am here to help you."

The government started messing with health insurance back when Lyndon Johnson came out with Medicare and Medicaid. That was supposed to solve the problems of the elderly and the indigent. What it did is drive the cost of medical care so high that many people that had insurance before could no longer afford it. Within a short time, health insurance became drastically more expensive.

I was selling health insurance at the time and we sold a basic hospital policy that covered a family of four for about 160 dollars per year. It was not all-inclusive but if you went to the hospital almost everything was covered. It did not cover doctor's visits in the office but a normal office visit was around $5 so almost anyone could afford to go to a doctor if they were seriously ill or injured.

Within a short time after the law went into effect, doctors started raising their rates drastically because they now knew that the government would pay whatever they charged as long as they charged everyone equally. Hospitals soon followed suit and my company Farmers and Traders Life Insurance Co. quit selling health insurance altogether.

Of course, I cannot say that sooner or later the cost of health care would not have risen to the levels it is today. I am sure other things played a part in the rising costs. Organ transplants were just becoming popular around that time. I am positive that drove up the cost of insurance as well.

One thing I am positive of is that we need one more law. It would read, "No bill may be enacted by Congress and signed into law by the President unless another law is repealed." Imagine how that would change the dynamic in politics. Now these evil and greedy souls that we call Representatives and Senators would have to give some thought to the process before putting forth their self-serving agendas.

For a while, that would be fairly easy. For example, in Arizona, there is a law making it illegal for a man to cut his own hair. I would think that would be a fairly easy one to repeal unless you were afraid of the "Barber's Union."

There are thousands of laws just as stupid as that one scattered throughout the country but eventually, they would have to start making some tough decisions.

Another thing I find ludicrous is that we have a "debt ceiling". It was enacted in 1917 and since that time, it has been raised 90 times. It has been raised 74 times since 1962. Now, what sense does it make to have a so-called ceiling if, at any president's whim, it can be raised?

I remember thinking something along those same lines when the National Basketball Association had what it called a "salary cap". It was set at 25 million dollars for an entire team's salaries but Michael Jordan was making 26 million dollars all by himself. I thought he should have had to take a million-dollar pay cut and play one-on-twelve.

Today our National Debt is so high that the only sensible solution would be to turn over the monopoly table and play a new game with one rule change. We need a balanced budget amendment to the Constitution saying that our government could never again spend more money than they collect, in revenues.

But then I am sure there would always be some exception that would come along. Perhaps some natural disaster would befall a section of the country or heaven forbid we decide to get into another large-scale war. Then certainly we would have to borrow money to pay for them right? Maybe a better idea would be to have enough budget excess in normal years to pay for the shortfalls in those lean years. That is what a responsible individual or family would do.

One thing having to do with politics today that drives me to distraction is that if you disagree with our present President you have to be a racist. I disagreed with every president we have had in my lifetime. Did that make me a racist? Of course not it made me human.

Of course, now I have to throw in my thoughts on political correctness. I find it ludicrous that we constantly have to keep changing our language in order not to hurt someone's feelings. It won't be long before Cleveland will have to change the name of its baseball team, and Washington will have to change the name of its football team. Revised note: Washington did eliminate the name Redskins and now calls themselves The Washington Football Team. One update is that the Washington Football Team became the Washington Commanders. And the Cleveland Indians will be called the Cleveland Guardians. Maybe even the birds will get angry because Baltimore calls itself the Ravens.

How long will it be before other teams are forced into political correctness? The Atlanta Braves is one team that comes to mind.

Why do we call people of color, African Americans? Most of those folks have never even been to Africa. And they are so far removed from their ancestors that might have come from there, they would need someone to help them research their family tree to get back that far. Calling them African American would be like calling me German American because at some point so far back I don't know about it, my Father's ancestors emigrated here from Germany.

And don't even get me started on the word "Gay". Those folks are not a bit happier than I am.

Chapter Thirty-Three Things That Have Happened in My 70 Plus Years

The Atomic Bomb

Although war was nothing new to the world, it changed in August of the year after I was born. Two atomic bombs were dropped on the country of Japan killing over 129,000 people and probably causing the death of many thousands more. This led to the end of the Second World War but started a "Cold War" that lasted until Ronald Regan's presidency. Everyone was convinced that a Nuclear Holocaust would obliterate us all and building bomb shelters became a lucrative business. I think it also contributed greatly to the drug problem that still haunts us today. Because many people thought that their deaths were imminent, they adopted an "eat, drink, and be merry" attitude. This got even worse during the Vietnam War that began in 1964.

Television

Television became a common household item. Although television was invented in 1927 many years before I was born, it did not become commonplace in mainstream America until after that. I was six or seven years old before we got our first black-and-white television. I remember my mother watching Kate Smith in the afternoon before we ate dinner each weekday. There wasn't much for us kids to watch at that time and so I don't think that either my brother or myself got real excited about it. Instead, we listened to the radio to such shows as The Lone Ranger. My father loved to listen to Amos and Andy but I never could quite grasp why.

Today most people could not imagine living without several TV sets in their houses. Some call it the idiot box and for the most part, they are right. You don't need to exercise any brainpower to sit and watch inane scenes acted out by people that have little talent for acting.

The Telephone

The telephone completely changed during my life. I can't remember a time when we did not have a telephone but it was a big ugly black thing that hung on the kitchen wall. It was a rotary dial and if your finger slipped you had to start over. We had a party line where 8 people shared one connection. I think we must have had a distinctive ring but I don't remember that for sure. I do know that people could listen in on your conversations, however. Our telephone number only had 5 digits. We did not have an area code to dial. Long-distance calls could only be made by dialing the operator and having her put the call through via a switchboard. We still had that old phone when I went into the Navy in 1962.

I don't remember exactly when we got our first touchtone phone but it was sometime after I got married and had my own house.

The first car phones were invented sometime around 1928 but they did not become in use until much later than that. I remember when I used to read Dick Tracy comics and he would use his two-way wrist radio and I thought how cool that would be to have.

But it wasn't until around 1983 that wireless technology came to the common person and even then you had to be a little richer than common to own and use one.

Those first car phones were huge and took up half of a normal car's trunk and required a huge antenna to be mounted on the outside of the vehicle. Only government people or doctors or lawyers could afford to use one as the airtime was charged at exorbitant rates. The phone itself cost well over $5,000.

Those phones were still around when I started selling phones in the mid-1990s as were what they called bag phones. Small handheld models were just becoming popular but a lot of people still wanted the full 3-watt telephones which could only be had in phones permanently mounted in the car or built into a bag. .6 watts was the maximum allowed for any phone that was held up to the ear because of the radiation and the danger of brain cancer.

When I began selling wireless phones we did so with the understanding that they would be used in dire emergencies only. At a cost of $1 per minute, the common person could afford to use the phone if they broke down along the highway or had some other emergency. Few people at that time ever envisioned what would happen with those phones in the coming years. Texting was just getting started at that time but it was hard to sell someone on the need for a texting package to their' rate plan.

And nobody dreamed that they would someday be able to play games, watch videos or television or read books on their wireless telephones.

Video Games

Imagine talking to a teenager today and trying to explain that when you grew up you did not have a television, a wireless telephone, or any kind of video game. And more unbelievable than that if you wanted to read something you had to have a book made out of paper. I guess it could be worse. The book could have been made from papyrus. By the time, I was a teenager I did go to what was called a pinball arcade but that was all they had were pinball machines. The bars had bowling machines where you slide a metal disc down an alley to knock down pins and occasionally you even found the ones that you bowled with a hard rubber ball.

Around the early 70s, we got our first Atari machine so I was nearly 30 years old before I ever played a video game. The only game we had with that early machine was pong shortened I guess from ping pong. We thought it was the greatest invention ever.

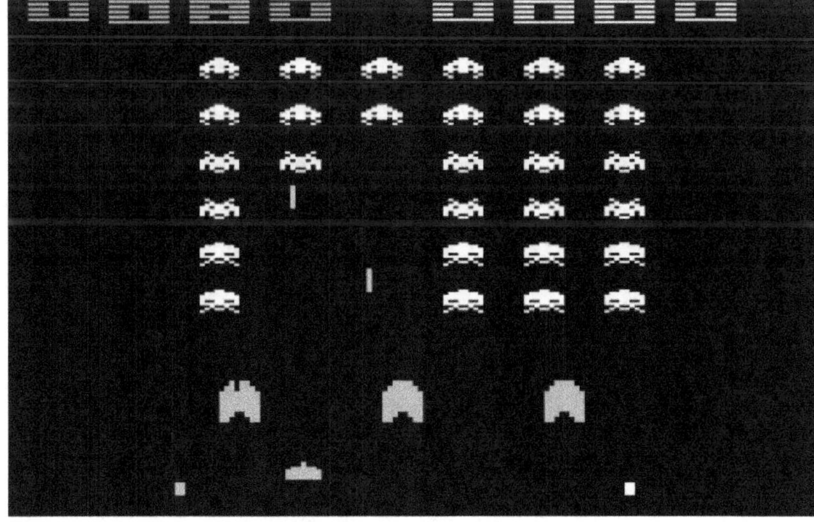

Then along came "Space Invaders" and we were mesmerized as those alien ships kept moving down to eventually blow up your mother ship.

Not long after we got Galaga and then Pac-Man and Ms. Pac-Man. Wow, we had so many different games that we didn't know which one to play. But still, we never dreamed of the interactive, Internet games that are available today. I guess that is why many youngsters no longer have the desire to read.

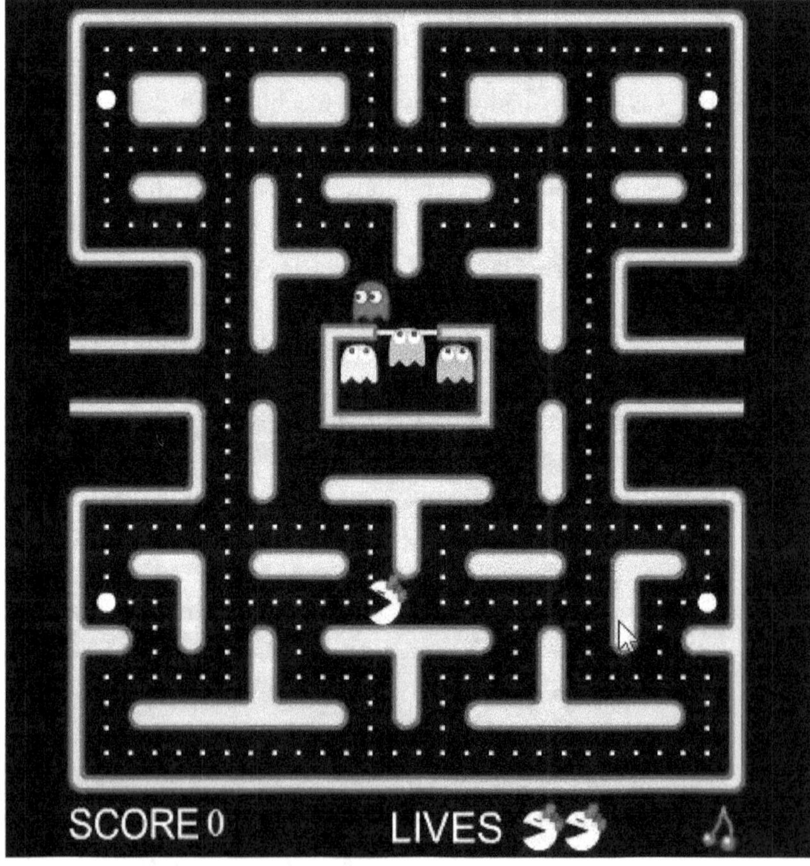

Satellite and Cable Television

I knew nothing of satellite television until somewhere around the mid-1980s. That came about because my partner in disorganized crime was trying to sell a large dish his father was manufacturing for around 10 thousand dollars. I thought that people would have to have more money than brains to pay that kind of money just to watch television.

At some point, another person who was heavily into electronics asked me if I thought I might be able to manufacture a satellite down converter. I looked at the design and it seemed simple enough so I told him I believed that I could but that I would need a dish set up at my home so that I could test and tune the units. So one day he arrived with this huge 8-foot diameter dish on the back of his pickup truck. It took four of us to carry that solid aluminum dish into my backyard and mount it on a metal pole that we had previously put into the ground in concrete.

He had a good idea of where the various satellites were on the horizon and so it did not take him too long to get the dish aimed properly. There were eight channels broadcast on that one bird. If you wanted to watch a different satellite you had to have someone watch the screen as you went out into the backyard and turned a crank that moved the dish to a different location.

In those early days, none of the signals were scrambled so you could watch anything that was up there. For me, the best part of having that dish was that I could find WPIX out of New York and watch the Yankee games.

Of course, that did not last long as soon the broadcasters decided that they needed to scramble their signals to keep freeloaders from watching their programming for free. Of course, that never made sense to me when you were dealing with advertiser-supported stations like WPIX or WGN or any of the other stations that sold advertising to pay for their service. You would have thought that the more people that watched the better but I am sure it was the cable companies that forced them to scramble their signals.

Of course, the folks on my side of the fence quickly learned of ways to unscramble said signals.

Then the big dishes began to disappear as the small ones came into being; put out by Dish Network and Direct TV. I never got involved in those even when we tried selling their services out of our kiosk in Wal-Marts, Sam's Clubs, and Costco. I did not like the sneaky way they tried to sell their services. They would offer a low price, to begin with, make you sign a two-year agreement with them, and then double the price after the first year. Of course, Cable Companies do the same thing today except most of them do not have a two-year agreement. In many instances, they have a monopoly so it doesn't matter if they have a contract with the customer or not.

When I was living in Phoenix the last time I cut the cord and went back to a regular antenna. I got 32 channels with nothing more than a set of rabbit ears that sat atop my TV set. I did need a digital converter though as my old TV was analog. I signed up for DSL and was able to add NetFlix to the mix and I had more television viewing than I could ever watch.

At some point, I am reasonably sure that cable will price itself out of the market although where we live now it is difficult to get more than 18 channels. The other channels are so low-power that you would have to live within a few miles of the tower to pick them up.

Sports

As I have mentioned earlier I loved baseball. April 1st was one of the best days of the year for me because it was the opening day of the baseball season. I didn't pay too much attention to football or basketball until much later in my life.

One thing that we did watch was Friday Night at the Fights. That was the only sporting event that my father ever seemed to care much about. And of course, everyone knew who the heavyweight champion of the world was and most people knew who the middleweight and welterweight champions were as well.

I remember the controversy when Cassius Clay knocked out Sonny Liston to become champion. I watched that fight and I swore that

Liston was scared to death before the fight ever began. For a big bruising thug of a man, that was hard for me to believe. Many people thought that the fight was rigged including Floyd Patterson who had lost the title to Liston. His words were something like this: "Some people say he never hit him but I know he did. It was a short right hand and in my opinion, it would not have hurt a flea."

But regardless in the years that followed Clay or later Mohammed Ali did more for the sport of boxing than almost anyone that had come before him. He made a living with his mouth and with his fists and every time he fought the crowds watching grew.

I continued to watch boxing even when most of the big fights moved to HBO but once they began only showing them on pay-per-view, I gave up on the sport. I swore that eventually, the sport would die out because the young kids coming up as fans would not be able to watch it. And I think today that I was right. I do not know who the heavyweight champion is nor have I known for years. I see blurbs on Yahoo Sports now and again about some fight but not enough that anyone would care.

I guess the big thing today is Ultimate Fighting but that does not interest me in the least.

I first became interested in basketball when I moved to Olean, New York. The college there is St. Bonaventure and at the time, they had just recruited a big center by the name of Bob Lanier. The entire town was crazy about that team and many of us thought they had a great chance to become national champions.

They did get to the semi-finals one year but Lanier had got hurt in the quarter-finals and that ended any real chance they had to win it all.

That got me started and I began to watch pro ball as well. Again I picked a New York team, the Knicks to root for. When I moved to Phoenix many years later I started rooting for the Phoenix Suns and we even went to see them play. The cost of a ticket was around $8 and you paid another $2 to park. So it was no more expensive to go to a game than to go out to a bar and have a few drinks and about the same as going out to a mediocre restaurant for dinner.

But all that has changed. First, you cannot root for a player anymore the way I did for Mickey Mantle. These guys move around wherever the money is. They have no loyalty to a team. Their only loyalty is to their wallets.

We did go to a Cincinnati Bengals football game the year before last. Two tickets were $120 and it was $50 to park in a lot three blocks from the stadium.

Maybe that is the way it should be. After all, we live in a capitalist country. But I will tell you I no longer watch basketball and I no longer watch baseball. I do watch football although after seeing the cheating that went on this past year I may give that up as well. I do watch golf and although I think the prize money is ludicrous I am not so adamantly opposed to it, as I am the salaries in the other sports. My reasoning is, at least, they have to play well to get paid. That is something that other sportspeople do not have to do. Once they have a huge salary they can get fat and happy not caring if their team wins or not.

I used to love college football. Every year on New Year's Day you could watch several different bowl games on network TV. But even that has disappeared as the colleges have let their greed push all the games onto cable for a bigger payday.

And without cable, most of the March Madness basketball tournament is unavailable to you.

Money has ruined sports.

Methods of Farming

While the picture below is not of our family barn it is a close replica. It gives one an idea of the scope of the old family farm.

When I was growing up most of the farms were small outfits. Our farm had 224 acres and we milked about 35 head of cows.

In the early years, though we did own a big old Massey Harris tractor, a team of horses did most of the work. They were far from a matched team as one was a huge black horse and the other a like-sized red horse. The tractor got its share of work during the summer but in the winter and early spring, those horses did the lion's share of the work. You see horses rarely got stuck in the mud but tractors did. It was a common sight to see those two big horses pulling the manure spreader or plowing or dragging the plowed fields.

And speaking of spreading manure for most of my youth that spreader had to be loaded by hand. Every day Dad would back it into the barn and with pitchforks and shovels, we would load it. Later he did get an automatic gutter cleaner that scrapped the manure out of the gutters and up a conveyor and dumped it into the spreader automatically.

Of course, the calf pens still had to be cleaned manually. That was the slinkiest task I ever did.

I don't ever remember having to milk the cows by hand but I did see Dad do it a few times for one reason or another. Most of the time we used milking machines and emptied the milk into pails to be carried several hundred feet up across the road to be put into milk cans which we put into a large cold water tank for keeping until the milk truck came by to pick them up in the morning.

There was a great advantage of having that milk in those cans, though. We always had sweet cream to put on our oatmeal in the morning. And it made great whipped cream as well.

After a while, Dad did build a milk house next to the barn so that the pails did not have to be carried quite so far and finally he put in a pipeline that connected directly to the milking machine and transferred the milk to a large cooled vat inside the new milk house.

If my father could see this he would roll over in his grave.

I am sure today all those things are completely primitive to the huge dairy complexes that have taken the place of the small dairy farm I was used to.

This picture is more like what a farm would look like today.

Automobiles

Massive changes have taken place in the auto industry during my lifetime. Ascetic changes may have been more pronounced between the time that Henry Ford started his assembly line up until I was born than afterward but the way cars are serviced and worked on has changed tremendously. Earlier I mentioned having a 1954 Ford, which had an oil seal go out ruining the pistons and crankshaft. Other than having the block rebored my father and I did the entire job ourselves. And for most of my life most common repairs like changing spark plugs or brake pads, I did myself.

Not too long ago our Saturn Station wagon began acting up and I suspected that it was not firing on all cylinders. So we took it to a Chevy dealer to have it serviced. Sure enough one of the cylinders was not firing. Imagine my shock and dismay to find that you had to disassemble the entire head of the motor just to get at the spark plugs. The cost of the repair was over 500 dollars.

Then I recently took my daughter's van in to have the brake pads replaced only to learn that you no longer can replace just the brake pads, you have to change the rotors at the same time because they make the rotors out of the same composite material as the brake pads to save weight in the vehicle. When the pads wear down so do the rotors.

The fuel pump went out in the Saturn this last week. I figured how bad could it be, just get an external electric pump and bypass the one in the tank. Nope, you can't do that with these new cars. $728 later the car is back on the road.

They have engineered these newer cars (I haven't bought a brand-new car since 1981) so that you can no longer do most of the mechanical repairs yourself. I sometimes wonder how AutoZone stays open.

And now the climate nazis are pushing us to buy enormously priced electric cars. While that makes little sense because the manufacture of the batteries does more harm to the environment than the burning of gasoline, yet someone in the government is obviously making huge money off of electric vehicles. Any time when the government tries to get you to do a specific thing, follow the money and you will know why.

E-Readers

I grew up with a natural love of reading. As mentioned earlier, we did not have television, personal telephones, or video games in our earliest years. What we did have were books, many of them of the religious variety but it was something to do. And once I started school I had access to the library where countless adventures were just waiting for me to check out.

Some of my favorite authors at that time were Jim Kjelgaard, Jack London, and Bruce Catton who wrote mostly civil war stories. I was fascinated with anything dealing with the great outdoors or history. I read everything that I could get about the American Revolution, the early settlers like Daniel Boone and Davy Crocket, and also about the Civil War. I still find that period of our country to be spellbinding.

Later I started to read mysteries and when I got into high school even somewhat enjoyed the writing of Shakespeare. One of my favorite required readings would have been Edgar Allen Poe. If you want Macabre writing none could be better than Poe.

The strange thing was that once I graduated from high school, I never again had a library card until a year or so ago.

I subscribed to Reader's Digest and bought tons of Reader's Digest Condensed Books. I also subscribed to many different magazines.

I have no idea how much money I have spent on books over the years but I do know that at some point buying even paperbacks became quite expensive. I just saw an advertisement for a C.J. Box book that in paperback they wanted $23.95 for.

This brings me to my all-time favorite invention, The Kindle, e-reader. My children gave me my first Kindle for my birthday perhaps 7 or 8 years ago. I quickly fell in love with the fact that if I wanted a book I could just purchase it and it would miraculously appear on my

Kindle. Most of the books I purchased were much cheaper than buying paper books, many around 5 or 6 dollars.

And then I discovered something unbelievable. Many new authors were giving their books away for free. So I would spend an hour or so each day searching for those free books and downloading everyone that did not have a cost. At some point, I quit doing that. I now have over 4000 books in my library and although there are usually over 24000 new free books per day, I have more than I can ever read at my fingertips.

What I did do however is get a library card so that I can read some of the better-known authors who still charge far more than I want to spend for even their ebooks. And this can be done from the comfort of my own home and have them sent directly to my Kindle as well. For instance, I have now read almost the entire series of Joe Pickett novels by CJ Box. Instead of paying over 23 dollars per, I have spent nothing.

Flipping Houses

The first house that Janice and I owned was a little two-story house in Olean, New York. It had hardwood floors throughout and a fairly nice kitchen. There were two bedrooms upstairs and one downstairs that we later converted into a beauty shop. My parents gave us 1,000 to put down and the mortgage on the balance came to $65 per month including taxes and insurance. I owned a brand new Mustang Fastback that I was paying $75 per month on. I only made around $80 per week after taxes so our budget was pretty tight. However many years ago we did find a budget we had drawn up for that year and we had allocated $12 per week for groceries. Of course, we ate an awful lot of spaghetti made from ground beef from a cow that my folks had slaughtered and canned tomatoes that came from Janice's folks.

I can't remember our reasoning for wanting to sell that place but I do know that when we started looking for another house we drove on a road between Portville, New York, and Cuba, New York, and Janice remarked, "I would not live in this God-Forsaken area." So guess where we ended up buying our next house?

It was an old farmhouse in a little dot on the map called Obi, New York. It came with six acres of land for a whopping price of $8500. We could have had the barn and all 200 acres for $12,500 but I didn't think I had any use for that much land. I regretted it several years later when the barn and acreage sold for over 40,000.

There were two main drawbacks to the house. First, the kitchen had old white cupboards that made it look run down. And secondly, the floors were old plain linoleum. We had two choices we could either put in wall-to-wall carpeting or we could put in hardwood flooring. We decided to go with the latter and purchased some 3/4 inches of white oak flooring. Man did those floors look sharp when they were finished. We also paneled the walls, lowered the ceilings, and installed indirect lighting. Electrical outlets were built into the hardwood flooring, at least, two on every wall.

We remodeled the kitchen with new cupboards. I think it cost us around 1200 dollars for the cupboards and we installed them ourselves.

At some point, I learned how to become a chimney builder. I grew up in a house heated by wood and so I figured I could save some money by using a Franklin stove as a secondary heat source. At first, we just ran a regular stovepipe through the wall not realizing that was a very bad idea. One fall I fired up that stove and immediately heard a swooshing sound. When the pipe began glowing and the wind cap melted off and fell onto the roof, I called the fire department. Of course, everything was out by the time they got there but a valuable lesson was learned, build a real chimney.

Water for the house was supplied by a spring that sat up on the side of a hill behind the house. Because the water traveled so far downhill we had tons of pressure. Our neighbors ran cattle directly behind that spring so they had to be fenced off from getting into it. One thing we could not keep out, however, were snakes, and once when our water pressure died we had to pull a dead snake out of the line. After that, we installed a better filter on the far end of the pipe.

I also learned that you had to leave the water dripping in the winter. One morning we got up and there was no water. I quickly figured out that the line had frozen and was probably under the house. So with my trusty flashlight and a butane torch, I crawled down and started to heat the line. Of course, when it finally melted it sprayed water all over me so I was half-frozen by the time I got back inside.

I truly believe that was the best house that we ever lived in. Not so much perhaps because of the house itself though that was a big part of it because it had everything that I liked surrounding it.

Directly behind the house was a stand of thorn apple trees where partridge and cottontail rabbits abounded. And whitetail deer were prevalent as well. The only thing that we lacked was a good place to fish although there was a creek that ran along the base of a huge hill across the road from the house. It got pretty dry most summers though so fish did not do well in it.

In 1974, we sold that house for 23,500 and moved to Malone, New York.

The next house was a disaster like none you could imagine. It was way out in the country in a little berg called Constable. I paid 15000 dollars cash for that place so that we would not have to pay a mortgage payment. I think when we finally sold it we about broke even.

I only owned three other houses in my life after that. One in the City of Malone that we got with an FHA mortgage for I believe $27000. One in Glendale, Arizona that we paid $47000. And the last one in Phoenix, Arizona that we paid $92000 for.

Out of all those houses, the one that was probably the best was the first one that we bought for 5500 dollars in Olean, New York.

Every once in a while, my wife will be watching the home and garden channel on cable and I will hear someone say that they budgeted 500,000 to buy a house and another 100,000 for renovations and I think, for a half-million, I should be able to get a house that does not require renovations. You would think that a half-million-dollar house should be a mansion but they aren't. They are just regular run-of-the-mill houses that I could have bought when I first started for less than 10,000.

The Internet

Not long ago I heard someone say "What did we do before the Internet?" My reply was that we had things called dictionaries and encyclopedias. I remember just after we had gotten married an encyclopedia salesman came to our house and talked us into getting the complete set. It was 27 volumes and every year you had to buy an addendum. And we had a couple of huge dictionaries as well.

If you were wondering about something that had happened years before you could attempt to look it up once you found the correct volume. If it was something more recent however you might have to go to the library and look through their newspaper files. Or go to the newspaper itself and look through past issues.

Doing a term paper or just a school assignment could take hours or days even just to research the paper.

All that changed when the World Wide Web came along. I am not going to try to explain how it works or even why it began. If you want to know those things you can look them up on the Internet.

What I will say is that it has made things much easier for students and educators alike. And as an author, I am eternally grateful every time I have to look something up for one of my books.

There are thousands if not millions of other things that can be done because of the Internet.

Computers

I think in this category, calculators must be included. I remember in high school we had a math teacher try to explain the workings of a slide rule and every student was required to purchase and learn to use one. I don't think I ever mastered the art but it was the first time that I saw something other than a pen and paper used to figure out a mathematical problem. I guess I would have been completely shocked if he had made us use an abacus.

I was out of school before I saw my first calculator. I used one in the insurance business to figure out premiums and to show cash values to the customer.

I imagine about that time many students were thinking they no longer had to know how to add, subtract, multiply, or divide since they could just use their calculators to get the correct answer. I saw a cartoon about that one time of a teacher standing up in front of the class with a calculator in her hand, shaking her head no and the caption read, "Because batteries go dead. That is why."

The first real computer that I ever owned was a Tandy that I got from Radio Shack. It had 16 kb of memory and I think that was an upgrade from the basic unit. I don't remember ever being able to do anything with that machine.

I was getting into writing about that time and so I purchased another computer, this one with a 20-megabyte hard drive that the salesman told me would be more memory than I would ever need. Of course, that was before I knew anything about The Internet.

I am sure that computers have made life easier for many people but I am equally sure that they have caused as many or more problems than they have solved. Children today spend almost all their time playing some type of game on their computer instead of interacting with others, reading, or playing outside.

Artificial Intelligence

As of this revision, there is a big controversy about artificial intelligence. To hear some people one would think that the Cylons from Battlestar Galactica are ready to eminently attack Earth. This topic came up because of a new app called ChatGBT. And while this app is new the idea is not. We have had Artificial Intelligence for a long time. Most car companies, use robots to do welding and other assembly tasks.

The grocery stores are using self-checkout stands. Our computers are a form of Articficial Intelligence. It has been a long time since IBM's Big Blue beat a human chess grandmaster.

If you have ever used Spellck or Grammarly or any other grammar program, you have used artificial intelligence.

The fear is that these programs are becoming so sophisticated that they will soon replace human beings. And they may be right about that but remember the grocery stores have been replacing human labor with self-checkout stands for a long time.

I know that some songwriters and authors are concerned that artificial intelligence will be able to do their jobs better than they can. That would not surprise me considering some of the so-called music and literature that is being produced today by humans.

I guess we will just have to wait and see what the final result will be. Hopefully, it will not be "The Cylons are coming.:

Big Box Stores Did Not Exist

Twice a year my mother would drive us to Jamestown, New York to go shopping. Each of those times she would take us to a Sears-Roebuck Store. One of those trips was to get school clothing and it usually occurred in August. Most of the time we were allowed two sets of clothes but it was expected that the second set was only in case something unusual occurred. If at, all possible we wore one set of clothes for the entire school week.

Most items that you needed to buy had their separate store that you went to.

But around 1962 things began to change when Sam Walton opened his first store. In the early days, Walton had a master plan. He would put a small Wal-Mart into each town he expanded to. He would lower prices to the point where he drove all the small merchants out of business and then he would close those small stores and set up one somewhere between towns. Since everyone else was gone the people had no choice but to drive the extra miles and buy from his stores.

In 1970, Walmart became publicly traded and I kick myself to this day for not buying that stock. A few hundred dollars in Wal-Mart stock in 1970 would be worth a small fortune today.

Of course, other people tried to capitalize off of Walton's idea but none was even close to as successful as he was. Today Walmart is the largest employer in the United States. Note: As of the summer of 2021 Amazon has passed Walmart as the largest employer.

Home Owner's Associations and Zoning Boards.

When I was growing up if you owned property, what you did with it was your own business. If you didn't keep up the lawn or you had too much trash around the property, your neighbors would figure that you had some type of problem and would stop by and offer to help you.

Today they wouldn't bother with that, they would just call the zoning commission or the homeowners association and have you ticketed.

I believe that if you buy a property and pay your taxes you should be able to do what you want with it within reason. Of course, keeping a neat yard is a good thing but having someone tell you what color you can paint your house or what type of fence is required is beyond my comprehension. Who says that having every house look identical to the one next to it is for the good of the neighborhood? For heaven's sake, we drinkers might not be able to tell which house we should be sleeping in.

I remember the first time that I ran afoul of the zoning commission. I purchased a house in Glendale, Arizona for $47,000. At some point, we decided to add a tool shed to the house. We checked the zoning rules and found out that we could have a freestanding shed added to the property as long as the total area of the roof was not more than 200 square feet. In effect, that would be 10 by 20. We also wanted to enclose a back patio to make it what they called an Arizona room.

We didn't put in any electrical wiring so there were no safety concerns.

At that time, my oldest son also had an old Mustang that he was restoring which he had parked in the side yard. That was the only thing that I believed we would be in violation of. And zoning laws also stated that the car would not be in violation as long as it was completely covered.

Unfortunately, the zoning people showed up one day when the car was not covered and found that the license was expired. As long as they were writing the citation they figured they might as well write one saying that the back porch was in violation and that the tool shed needed to be removed.

I wrote a letter to the City of Glendale and tried to explain that we were not in violation but all that got me was a subpoena to show up in court. Before my court date, the City Attorney called me into his office and told me that if I would remove the vehicle, tear down what we had done to the back porch and remove the tool shed that they would drop the charges.

I told them the vehicle was already gone but I was not going to do the other two things because I believed that they were not in violation of the code. So they decided to prosecute me.

On the day of my court hearing, I asked my son to show up to testify that the area of the roof of the shed was under the 200 square feet that were allowed.

The zoning guy testified as to what he thought was wrong with the addition of the shed stating that it was not freestanding and the roof appeared to be over the 200 square feet that were allowed. On cross-examination, I asked him if he had ever been in that shed. His answer was no. I asked him how close he had come to that shed and he remarked that he had only seen it from the street.

I also asked him if he had ever inspected the enclosed back porch and his answer was the same.

"So let me see if I understand what you are saying," I began. "You have never been in the shed nor have you ever measured the roof, so I assume you have no direct knowledge of what you are testifying here today?"

He then stated that even if I was right about the size of the roof the storage shed was still too close to the property boundary and so needed to be moved.

My rebuttal was that may or may not be true but that is not what you cited me for, is it?

He sheepishly answered no.

When they finally rested their case, I called Robert to the stand and asked him if he had ever measured the roof of the storage shed. He answered that he had and that it was just under the 200 square feet that were allowed. The district attorney then tried to get him to say that the shed was not freestanding but without success. Robert simply stated that he had never seen where it was attached to the main building. She then started to ask him about the back porch.

Well, I had seen enough Perry Mason episodes to know that you shouldn't be asking things on cross-examination that were not covered by direct so I stood up and yelled, "I object on the ground that was not covered under my direct examination." I think it was all the judge could do to keep from laughing at that point as she said, "Overruled."

When Robert finished his testimony I stood up and said, "I rest my case."

The judge looked at me and said, you don't mean that you rest your case. Surely you are going to testify?"

I said, "No, your honor. I don't need to testify, the City failed to prove their case."

That shocked the District Attorney because she felt sure that she would get me on the stand and she would force me to testify against myself.

The judge left the room to consider what she had heard and when she came back she found me not guilty on the charge of the storage shed and not guilty on the charge of the back porch. She did fine me $125 for having the car uncovered on the side lawn. The District Attorney was furious and I thought her head would explode.

The judge called me up to her bench. She said, "You did a reasonably good job of defending yourself in my court. However, I doubt that they are done with you yet. So if they do come after you again, I suggest you hire a lawyer."

They never did come back. I guess getting beat by a common everyday citizen was enough for them.

I know there are a lot of people that agree with zoning laws. They feel that we need the government to make sure that every single thing we do in our lives is regulated.

As for me, I take the Daniel Boone approach. He said, "If you can see the smoke from your neighbor's chimney you live too close."

So many things have changed during my lifetime and I would probably be shocked if I could see what will happen in the next 70 years. I doubt however that anything that can happen will be as drastic a change as what has happened in the past 70.

Chapter Thirty Four-Update December 2022

It is hard to believe that I originally wrote this book 8 years ago. So many things have happened since then that I feel the need to update it

Janice and I have moved twice since then. The first time was at a retirement apartment complex in Cincinnati, Ohio. We lived there for three years and were fairly happy there except for some neighbors that complained about noise every time our granddaughter would come to visit. The floors were not properly installed and if you just walked across them it would make noise. Imagine how much more noise a three-year-old can generate.

We had moved originally from Phoenix to Amelia, Ohio to help our daughter with her son that had a rare disease. It is called esophageal esophagitis or EE for short. It is caused by white blood cells attacking the digestive process. I had never heard of it before Johnnie was diagnosed with it. I wonder if it is something new or if it has always been around but not diagnosed. Many years ago, children died for something they labeled as a failure to thrive.

Cincinnati Children's Hospital was one of the only places in the country where that disease could be treated and so Autumn packed up her family and moved from Oklahoma to Amelia where she bought a house. Janice and I packed up our things and moved to join her so that she would have someone to watch the boy while she was working.

At some point when we figured that our help was less needed we moved to what we thought might be a quieter environment. At some point, the doctors at Cincinnati Children's decided that they had done as much as they could for Johnnie and so Autumn moved back to Mannford, Oklahoma where she had friends and other family.

Chapter Thirty Five-Politic Update

I would be remiss if I didn't mention the political changes that have occurred in the past 8 years. One of the biggest things that happened was that a businessman and reality television personality was elected President of the United States.

I have to tell you that I was not enthused when he decided to run for the office. There were other candidates that I felt were much better qualified, but once he won the nomination and Hillary Clinton became the Democrat candidate, I got behind him.

And while he had many flaws, I had to admit that he was the best President that I had seen in my lifetime and with few exceptions, probably was the best President in our history. I reason that he always put the best interest of the Country as his highest priority.

The preceding President had shown over and over again that he was ashamed of many aspects of the United States. In fact, his wife, Michelle said on the night he was elected that it was the first time in her life that she was proud to be an American. And the first thing that Obama did as President was to launch himself on an apology tour of the world.

Trump was totally different. He made no apology for his country. His campaign slogan was "Make America Great Again" and that was what he set out to do. He started to build a wall on our Southern Border to slow the influx of illegals into the country. When Mexico didn't want to do anything to help in that regard, Trump threatened to install sanctions against them and soon they came around to his way of thinking.

When Trump discovered that many of the countries of NATO were not paying their fair share, he put pressure on them to begin doing so.

Trump encouraged the oil companies to expand and to make our country energy independent. When he left office he had accomplished that goal.

Chapter Thirty Six- The Sabotaging of America

For years people have been pushing for a One World Government. I guess they spent too much time watching Star Trek and the fallacy of The United Federation of Planets. How they expect that all the different peoples of the world can get along enough to be governed by one entity is beyond me. After all people in this country cannot even get along. How do they expect the Arabs and Jews who have hated each other for thousands of years to all of a sudden submit to a common government?

That pipe dream had been put on hold because of Trump's America First policies. But truly bad ideas never really die. They just get recycled. But as long as Trump was in the way, the One World Government could not happen. So, they had to get rid of the man. Even before he was President they conjured up a phony Russian collusion story about him, hoping that would slow down the Trump train.

When that didn't work and he won the election (which they never truly acknowledged) they tried to impeach him because of a phone call he had with the Ukrainian President. When the Senate failed to convict him, one would have thought that they would give up. Not so.

Remember that the economy was so good that even he was a shoo-in for reelection. Unless of course something terrible were to happen.

To understand what happens next you have to piece together a couple of facts that the press won't cover. First Joe Biden has always wanted to be President but has run into a wall each time he has tried for the office. In the upcoming Presidential election, Biden would stand no chance against Trump because of the state of the economy.

Biden's son Hunter was selling his father's influence to Ukraine, Russia, and China. That influence would be bigger if Joe became President of the United States. Therefore it was in the best interest of Russia and China to help Biden with his candidacy. But, how could they do that?

Well, In China there was a bioweapons laboratory that was experimenting with making a Covid virus into a weapon of mass destruction. What better way to test it than to release it into the general population and then spread it to the entire world? It apparently worked because over 1 million Americans died from it.

So how does this fit into the Trump – Biden scenario? Well, before this deadly virus was released and brought to America Joe Biden could not have been elected as President of the United States. And thus his influence would have been worthless to the Chinese Communists. But once this virus hit our shores, the record economy of Donald Trump crumbled. This opened the way for Biden to gain a foothold back into politics. And of course, he blamed Trump for the virus although in all likelihood it was his son that asked the Chinese to release the deadly disease.

Even with this new development, Trump still would have won if the election was conducted fairly, but it was not. New rules were drafted allowing ballots to be counted that were not actually cast on Election Day. The theory was that it was too dangerous to have people go to the polls so they could just request a ballot, fill it out and send it in. That might have been alright if that was what happened. But the evidence is clear that ballot harvesting took place. In other words, the Democrats sent people out to nursing homes, senior residences, and other places where large numbers of people lived. They got those people to sign their names on ballots and then filled them out selecting Democrat candidates and especially Joe Biden.

How do we know that happened? Because when Trump was leading by thousands of votes in Pennsylvania, miraculously boxes of ballots were discovered and every one of them was supposedly for Joe Biden. No reasonable-minded person would believe that such a thing could happen, but it did. And it is important to remember that only a few thousand votes made a difference in the election.

So how does Russia fit into this sordid mess? While Trump was President, Russia and North Korea were relatively quiet. Little Rocket Man as Trump calls the North Korean dictator, quit his blustering and for most of Trump's Presidency didn't send any missiles beyond his borders. The Russian dictator Putin was quiet as well. But as soon as it appeared that Trump would no longer be President, Putin began massing troops on the Ukraine border. And then when it became clear that Biden wouldn't do anything, he invaded the country.

At this point, we must remember that Biden had declared war on petroleum. On his first day in office, he canceled the Key Stone Pipeline and stopped all drilling on public lands. The price of gasoline, diesel fuel, and natural gas began to skyrocket. It wasn't long before we had reached an all-time high in the price of those commodities. Now, with Russia's invasion of one of the larger producers of natural gas, the prices rose exponentially.

Of course, Biden now used Russia's invasion as an excuse for the high price of fuel. He called it "Putin's price hike".

Along with the price of gasoline, all other prices rose to all-time highs. Not too surprising since almost everything that we buy is delivered to us with gasoline or diesel engines. One would assume that Biden would have decided that Trump's energy independence would be the way to go, but not so. He doubled down on his war on fossil fuels. To try to offset the high price of gas, he decided to release oil from our strategic energy reserves, Those are supposed to be used in cases of emergencies. As of this update, our supply of oil is at an all-time low. We need to pray that we don't need that oil for something important,

Heaven forbid that one of our many enemies doesn't decide to attack us.

While inflation has become a huge problem in this country it is by far not the only one. While Trump was President, he had almost contained the influx of illegal aliens coming across our southern border. He did that by building a wall and by working with the Mexican government. He initiated a stay-in-Mexico policy whereby those seeking asylum would have to remain in Mexico while they were waiting for their asylum case to come up in the United States. Since the vast majority of asylum claims are bogus many of the people who would have otherwise come into our country, disappeared, and never show up for their hearings had to remain in Mexico for extended periods of time.

Biden ended that policy on his first day in office and stopped construction on the wall as well. The result has been a huge influx of illegals entering our country. It is estimated that over 5 million illegals have entered our country since Biden became President.

To put that into perspective we now have enough illegal immigrants in just those two years to fill Chicago, Illinois twice. Any reasonable person would agree that is not sustainable. Unfortunately, Joe Biden and his Democrat cronies are not reasonable people.

This creates a terrible burden on the municipalities that are trying to deal with this massive hoard. That burden fell mostly onto border communities until some of the Republican Governors decided to begin bussing a few to cities that claimed to be a sanctuary for foreigners. Of course, it would take a great many buses to handle the huge flow that is coming across our southern border.

But, it is not just the monetary problem that these people create. Since it is so easy for people to cross our border, drug smugglers are using them to transport illegal drugs into the country. One such drug is called fentanyl which has killed over 100,000 Americans this year alone. If a country allowed a bomb to be brought into the United

States that killed that many people we would declare war on such a country, but neither Mexico which allows the substance nor China which manufactures the drug are being held accountable. Again it is Biden's lax open border policy that is to blame.

Add to those problems an exponential increase in crime in Democrat-run cities. Somewhere along the way, the liberals in this country decided that we needed to revamp our criminal justice system to be fairer to the poorer population that had difficulty paying cash bail. So some District Attorneys decided not to ask for bail even in cases of violence. People who commit assaults, battery, and even rape are turned loose with no bail set. It got so bad that in Los Angeles, a recall petition was circulated to get rid of the District Attorney. Even though enough valid signatures were gathered the powers that be disallowed the petition.

In Philadelphia, the District attorney was just as bad but is still turning people loose to commit crimes again. The same thing is happening in New York City. What do those cities have in common? Democrat Mayors and Democrat Governors.

Because of all these many problems, it was forecast that in the 2022 general election, there would be a "red wave". But either the voters were stupid or the election was crooked because not only was there not a red wave, the Democrats actually picked up a seat in the United States Senate.

Unless something drastically changes in our election process I have little hope for my country.

Chapter Thirty Seven-A few posts from my Word Press Blog –Musings of a Baby Boomer

Feb. 18, 2016

The World has changed and not for the better

Hardly a day goes by that I do not hear my grandchildren ask their mother if they can go somewhere. Usually, I ask them why they want to go somewhere and their answer is always the same. We are bored.

I find that strange since they have I pads that are full of games and videos. They have stacks of books. They have toys that are too numerous to talk about but among them are bicycles and battery-powered scooters. They have television with the never-ending cartoon channel or the never-ending Sponge Bob channel. And if they tire of those, they have Netflix where they can watch power ranger, transformers, or if they are in a macabre mood, Goosebumps. And believe me, I have not even scratched the surface of the multitude of things they have to keep them entertained. Oh, I forgot, they have three dogs, two cats, a rabbit, a lizard, a tank of fish, and two turtles.

Now I think back to 1952 when I was about their age. We learned quickly that you did not say that you were bored around my parents. My mother's response was "If you are bored, I'll give you the board"> And believe me, you did not want the "board". Of course, my mother could tell just by looking at me if I was even thinking about being bored. It is amazing how much housework she could come up with to keep me busy.

And my father did not have to hear me say I was bored to find work for me to do around the farm. There were gutters to clean, animals to feed, and in the spring the dreaded calf pens to clean out.

Feb. 15, 2016

Our Country is in serious trouble.

With the death of Justice Scalia, we are at the crossroads of whether our country as we have known it for over 200 years will survive. As the court stands today there are 4 extremely liberal justices and 3 somewhat conservative justices and John Roberts. Scalia always voted to uphold the Constitution. Clarence Thomas usually voted to uphold the Constitution and the others vote will-nilly depending on how they felt the country is leaning at the time. If you doubt that just look at Robert's vote upholding Obamacare by using an argument that was not even put before him.

Some say that Obama should not nominate a replacement for Scalia. That is just crazy talk. Asking Obama not to nominate one of his liberal cronies would be like asking Satan not to offer a piece of fruit to a naked woman in a garden. He stated that he fundamentally wanted to change this country before he was elected president and he has done everything in his power to do just that. This is his best opportunity to make sure that the destruction of the country continues even after he has vacated the White House.

With another liberal on the court, he can almost guarantee that the second amendment will be scrapped and your guns are taken away. You can also be sure that no state will ever be able to put restrictions on the killing of babies in the womb or possibly even after they are born.

Now one would hope that since the Republicans control both houses of Congress that Obama would not be able to get a liberal justice approved. Unfortunately, I have watched Mitch McConnel and his lily-livered follower's knuckle under to Obama time and time again.

I am fearful for my country.

Never argue politics or religion

June 13, 2016

I tried to find who authored the above quote without success this morning. It came to mind because I allowed myself to become involved in a discussion about religion yesterday. For much of my life, I have managed to avoid such discussion although there was a period in my life when I preached the word of God with all the vehemence of a television evangelist. I never believed that I had all the answers but I believed that the religion I followed did. It was my opinion that the Elders were guided by the Holy Spirit much as the Catholics believed that the Pope was infallible for the same reason., Obviously, since my religion and Catholicism were diametrically opposed in our beliefs one or both of us must have been misinformed.

Now I must tell you that I do not doubt the existence of God. The universe and the things in it are far too perfect to have happened by accident. I however have my doubts about the accuracy of any organized religion. Now, don't get me wrong, much good is done in the name of religion. But on the other hand, many terrible things are done in that same name. For instance, during World War II Catholic priests in the United States were blessing the weapons of war that were created to kill people in Germany. At the same time, Catholic Priests in Germany were blessing the guns and bombs used to kill our soldiers. And from all accounts, both believed that God was listening to them.

During the Civil War,l Methodist preachers in the North were preaching about how it was the duty of all young men to go off and kill their countrymen in the South. At the same time, Methodist preachers in the south were preaching that it was the duty of all young men to go and kill those damn Yankees. Now supposedly they both believed in the same God so how was it that they were so opposed about that subject?

And so that brings about the question, why does God allow these things to be done in his name? That question is apropos today when people are butchering innocent men, women, and children in the name of Allah. Would you not think that Allah would smite them for using his name to justify such atrocities?

So perhaps I have a disagreement with the God that I do believe in. Why does he allow such terrible things to take place? Why does he allow the terrible illnesses that have cropped up in the last 50 years, many of which are aimed at the most innocent among us, young children? Surely an all-seeing all-powerful God could whisper in some scientist's ear the cure for these diseases. The scientist would simply go to sleep at night and wake up in the morning with the knowledge that if he just mixes strawberries with mint and feeds it to the populace that all diseases will be eradicated. So I have to wonder why God does not do that. Or perhaps he has and the scientist decided to discard the idea because he could not make any money off of curing a disease, that there was more money to be made out of selling drugs that only masked the symptoms.

But I guess I digress. The original post that I foolishly decided to put in my two cents on was about heaven and getting there through the belief in Jesus Christ. I simply asked if that is the case where did all the people go when they died before Christ came to earth to give his sacrifice? Now honestly I did not believe that anyone would give me an answer because unless you go back to God's original purpose for mankind, in Genesis there is no answer to be found in the scriptures. But low and behold someone actually did find an article written by a man that claimed he knew the answer.

So again I reiterate, never argue religion as there is no way to win since all religion is made up of some man's opinion. Now some of you will say that is not true, that their religion is based on the Bible and the Bible is the Word of God. And yet the Bible has been interpreted by millions of different people in different ways. That comes back to all religions are the opinions of man.

So in my attempt to show why you should never argue about religion, I have undoubtedly started another argument.

72 Virgins

June 16, 2016

Muslims are motivated to commit terrorism because the Quran tells them that fighting non-believers is a duty of every Muslim and the only way to be certain of going to heaven to enjoy untold sensual pleasures is to die fighting in the cause of Allah.

If they can make it to heaven, one of the rewards all Muslims are promised is 72 virgins.

Okay, so one of my questions is why only 72 virgins. Why not a thousand or a million? I assume that the reason for being surrounded by virgins is to have sexual encounters with them. The problem is that once you have sex with a virgin she is no longer a virgin and I guess would no longer be worthy of being part of the reward for killing innocent men, women, and children. So a motivated cowardly martyr could go through his reward in a month or so. Then is he left all alone or is he now surrounded by 72 women that are less than worthy of his attention? That sounds more like hell than heaven to me.

So now my second question is, more and more women are strapping on the suicide vests and making their way out to blow up people that choose not to live under Sharia law. So is their reward also 72 virgins? Since homosexuality is deserving of death under Sharia law, I assume that their virgins would be male. But that brings up a conundrum as well. How does the female martyr know that these males are virgins? Do you know how men lie when it comes to trying to get a woman into the sack? I imagine it would be pretty easy for 72 males to fool a female martyr into thinking that they are virginal.

I don't think these radical Muslim terrorists have thought this thing through very well. Perhaps they would be better off trying to live peacefully with their neighbors instead of killing them to get a questionable reward.

We are in grave danger

Aug. 2, 2016

Not since the election of 1860 has this country faced such a terrifying danger from an election. At that time the country stood on the precipice of a Civil War. Whether the country would remain one or end up divided was in the balance.

Today that choice pales in comparison with what will happen to our country after the November elections. For this election is not about what will happen in the next four years. It is not about who will occupy the White House for the next four years. But rather it is about who will sit on the Supreme Court for perhaps the next forty years. With the death of Anton Scalia, the court is presently split between four conservative justices and four liberal justices. And there is some question about how conservative John Roberts is.

The next president will break that tie. But that is not all that is at stake. Clarence Thomas has already announced that he will retire. That means that the next president will appoint at least two justices to the court. If it is Hillary Clinton the court will then be six liberals to three conservatives and every freedom that we hold dear will be gone. No one can doubt that with Clinton in the White House and a Liberal court, our right to bear arms will be taken from us. She has already said that she will limit the right to bear arms by executive order. Before Scalia's death, that order would not have stood. But with two more liberal justices on the court, no challenge to those types of orders would be upheld.

Clinton is also in favor of limiting the right to free speech. She wants laws passed that would make it a felony for anyone to speak out against the government's efforts to limit the use of fossil fuels. With a 6-3 liberal court those types of laws are bound to be found to be constitutional.

And once that happens is it really a stretch to see laws against any form of speech that criticizes Her Majesty Hillary? Surely no one would ever again be able to point out that she was taking bribes as part of her office.

Your right to practice your religion as you see fit will also disappear if you happen to believe that abortion is murder. Already the court has upheld some of the ridiculous requirements in The Affordable Care Act that mandate a business provide abortion drugs in their health insurance plans. And those decisions happened while Scalia was still alive. Just imagine how much worse it will be with a 6-3 liberal court.

And it is not just the Court that frightens me. Clinton has also said she intends to allow thousands of immigrants from Middle Eastern countries to enter our country. It does not take much of a stretch of the imagination to see scenes like what happened in Orlando all over the country. Radical Islamists will be in every state in the Union killing with impunity. And remember you will no longer have firearms for your own protection. How long do you think it will be before you are living under Sharia Law?

Please America, wake up before you elect another liberal as President. We cannot survive four years of Hillary Clinton and especially not forty years of the liberal Court she will appoint.

Looking back on that post and thinking about the past two years of Joe Biden is scary. How much trouble would this country be in if we had both Hillary and Creepy Uncle Joe in succession?

Professional Golfers are Pansies.

Aug 2, 2016

I know I have railed on this before but today I was watching the Olympics and the final round golf match. Before almost every shot someone, an official, or a caddy would say quiet in the gallery or no cameras, please. And of course, this is not an unusual happening. Now I don't know how much these spectators had to pay to get into the venue but I imagine over a thousand dollars.

For that amount of money, you would expect that you could comment on the action or perhaps take a picture. I can hear the outrage from you golfers. You have to understand the difficulty these shots are. Okay so let me get this straight. A person stands over an unmoving white ball, trying to hit it to a spot somewhere in a fairway that is 20 to 50 yards wide and you have to have total quiet to be able to do that.

Let's compare that with a baseball player trying to hit a ball that is coming at him at speeds nearing 100 miles per hour that is thrown from 60 feet 6 inches. And that ball is not coming in a straight line. It may move in towards him, out away from him, or straight down at the last moment. He has less than half a second to make up his mind to swing or hold up. And all this time the crowd is screaming at him and cameras are flashing everywhere. Have you ever heard an announcer at a baseball game say, no cameras please or quiet, please?

Or perhaps you might think about a quarterback in a football game. While moving to his left or right or backward or forward he has to throw a ball down the field at a moving target. Now in that case not only does he have to put up with crowd noise that reaches levels louder than a rock concert but he has to worry about having his head torn off by a charging lineman.

Or a visiting basketball player trying to make a free throw. Does the announcer ask for quiet and no movement behind the basket? No, they say "Noise Please" and the crowd is expected to make as much movement as possible to distract the player.

Now don't get me wrong, I do like to watch golf. But I think it would be less boring if when the player was lining up his putt they set off fireworks.

What Part of "The Green New Deal Could You Vote For?
Feb. 13, 2019

The vast majority of Democrats have signed on, at least in spirit, to The Green New Deal that was put forward by Ocasio Cortez recently. The question is how many of them will vote for it if it ever comes up in the House of Representatives or the United States Senate?

The bigger question is will the voters in this country support anyone that actually votes for such a bill? I would like to believe that the answer to that question is zero, but unfortunately, I have no such faith in the American electorate.

So let's take a look at what this proposed bill is designed to do. Its basic premise as I understand it is to greatly reduce carbon emissions in the United States Of course, since it is only aimed at our country the rest of the world would be free to pollute all they wanted. But I guess we have to start someplace.

To achieve that lofty goal, this idea (not yet a bill) would ban the use of 99% of all automobiles presently on the road within the next ten years. It would also ban the use of most airplanes including all passenger airplanes within the next ten years. Making that last ban viable would require the building of a massive high-speed rail system. If you believe that is a reasonable alternative to air travel you might realize that every place that has tried high-speed rail service has found that it is many times more expensive than was originally proposed. Even the ludicrous Governor of California just abandoned his hopes for the completion of their high-speed rail system between Los Angeles and San Francisco citing the tremendous cost of the project. Now imagine what the cost would be and the logistical problems would be if every city in California was to be linked to the system. In addition, consider how much private land would have to be taken from its owners by eminent domain to complete such a project.

And that is just in one state. Imagine if every city with an airport in the United States had to be linked together with high-speed rail. The mere idea is not just unreasonable, it is ludicrous. Maybe it could be accomplished in a thousand years but not in ten.

Banning all automobiles except for fully electric cars is almost as insane. Just the massive outlay of money that it would take to replace all the gasoline or diesel-powered vehicles would be astronomical. Sure the top 1% which the left is constantly vilifying might be able to afford to convert their vehicles to electric, but the cost would be prohibitive for the elderly and poor population that the left likes to pretend to protect.

But let's leave that for now and look at other parts of this pie-in-the-sky proposal. It also asks that all use of oil, natural gas, and nuclear power be done away with within ten years. One might wonder why they specifically want to outlaw nuclear power since it is one of the cleanest ways to produce power. And while they mention doing away with nuclear, there is no mention of doing away with coal. Amazing when you stop and think about it. I am sure that was just an oversight.

Now if you think that you can afford to convert or buy a new automobile that is 100% electric, can you also afford to replace your gas furnace, your gas hot water tank, your gas cooking stove, your gasoline-powered lawn mower, weed eater, and leaf blower? And of course, you would no longer have an alternate generator in case the electric power that keeps you warm or cool and allows you to cook your meals fails as we all know happens from time to time.

And don't forget that the unemployment rate will skyrocket when all those working in the petroleum industry no longer have jobs, not to mention those that work in related industries.

It is already estimated that the unemployment rate will climb to around 20% by the year 2030 because of advances in technology. We are seeing much of that when we go to the grocery store and see only one or two lanes open for those that refuse to use automated cashiers. How high will the unemployment rate be if The Green New Deal becomes a reality?

And they don't stop there. It seems they also take umbrage with cows and the fact that they fart methane gas. So to put a stop to that pollution they would mandate that all cows be slaughtered. But of course, they wouldn't stop there, pigs, horses, bison, elephants, deer, moose, caribou, and any other large animal would have to be killed to stop their polluting the planet.

I do hope that you are willing to become a vegan for there will be no meat to eat unless, of course, you become a cannibal. And that might not even be a viable alternative since they are suggesting killing not only babies but anyone that is over the age of eighty years old. And eventually, they would get around to culling the rest of the populations as well, in their attempt to save the planet from greenhouse gases.

Be honest do these ideas make sense to you? Pick even one of them and think about it seriously, can you honestly support such a thing? Now put all of these ideas into one bill and ask yourself how insane would a congressional delegate or Senator have to be to vote for the bill. But then again look at the morons that we have voted into public office. Is the idea so far-fetched?

The End.

I would like to thank you for reading this account of my life. If you would like to comment or make suggestions please write to me directly at waynesimmes@yahoo.com

Don't miss out!

Visit the website below and you can sign up to receive emails whenever Wayne Simmes publishes a new book. There's no charge and no obligation.

https://books2read.com/r/B-A-CQFL-KNTIC

Connecting independent readers to independent writers.

Did you love *I Never Thought I Would Live This Long*? Then you should read *I Wish I Was a Cowboy*[1] by Wayne Simmes!

[2]

A man dies and then comes back to life in a different time and different place. He soon discovers that he is in what he believes to be the old west, although he has no idea what territory or time frame he is in. He wonders how all this is possible, and then he meets a stranger that seems to be some type of guide.

---

1. https://books2read.com/u/meKowg

2. https://books2read.com/u/meKowg

Also by Wayne Simmes

The Devil, The Ghost and Will Anderson
I Wish I Was a Cowboy
I Never Thought I Would Live This Long

About the Author

I am an old farm boy from Western New York. I write a political blog on WordPress called Musings of a Baby Boomer. That name might be a little misleading because I was born before the end of World War II.

I have written Westerns, Mysteries and erotica under a Pen Name.